# PRAYING GOD'S WORD

## OVER YOUR CITY

### 40 DAYS OF PRAYER
TOWARD A TRANSFORMED COMMUNITY

Trey and Mary Anne Kent

PRAYERSHOP PUBLISHING

Terre Haute, Indiana

PrayerShop Publishing is the publishing arm of the Church Prayer Leaders Network. The Church Prayer Leaders Network exists to equip and inspire local churches and their prayer leaders in their desire to disciple their people in prayer and to become a "house of prayer for all nations." Its online store, prayershop.org, has more than 150 prayer resources available for purchase or download.

ISBN (Print): 978-1-970176-06-3
ISBN (E-Book): 978-1-970176-07-0

1  2  3  4  5 | 2025 2024 2023 2022 2021

# TABLE OF CONTENTS

# FOREWORD

Trey and Mary Anne have written a great resource for believers who desire to grow in their prayer lives. In *Praying God's Word over Your City*, they take us on an amazing 40-day journey of prayer that will lead to a transformed community.

I am so excited that God has led our dear friends to compile such a resource for the Church. Whether you are a long-time lover and practitioner of prayer or you are investigating prayer as a spiritual discipline to grow in, this book will be a great resource.

Each of the 40 days begins with a scripture, which is the call to and direction of the prayer action. I was encouraged to find the daily scripture first and foremost in the prayer guide. Following the scripture, is a brief summary of the day's prayer focus and a written prayer following the theme of the day. Their suggested prayer points calls the prayer warrior to turn these prayers in a very personal direction bringing them to a place of real-life application. Each day's prayer plan ends with a quote, related to the topic that is a memory hook for the rest of the day.

My wife, Julie, and I not only serve in the same city with Trey and Mary Anne, but enjoy doing life together with them in Austin and on mission trips around the world. In fact, along with a group of 20, the Kents and us took a trip to the Holy Lands in December of 2019. On that adventure, we chose to pray through our tour at locations where prayers were referenced in scripture. I love their application of praying scripture wherever they may be.

For the Kents, prayer is the focus of their lives and ministry. They minister in a non-denominational church setting, but have been used of God across denominational lines to lead in prayer events across the city of Austin for the past 20 plus years. Our Austin Baptist Association, which includes almost two hundred churches, has found a great friend and resource in Trey and Mary Anne. They regularly lead prayer conferences and retreats for us.

In *Praying God's Word over Your City*, you will experience a prayer guide written by a couple who live out daily their passion for the Church to become the house of prayer that God intended it to be.

David Smith
Executive Director, Austin Baptist Association

# INTRODUCTION

W hy pray for your city or community? That question is vitally important. In 2008, our lives were forever changed one night as we prayerwalked through our neighborhood at 12:30 am. Standing under a light pole in our suburb of Austin, the Lord spoke that he wanted his city covered in prayer night and day until Jesus returns!

Overwhelmed is an understatement of how we felt. Yet, after 12 years of helping to lead 100 churches to pray night and day for our city, one thing has become abundantly clear: God wants his cities prayed for by everyday Christians like us!

You may be a pastor or prayer warrior who leads a church, churches, or a prayer group. This book would be a great tool to mobilize your church or community to begin to pray in unity for 40 days or on a weekly or monthly basis.

If your church participates in the America Prays mobilization plan that unites churches to pray 24/7 for their city (See Afterward on page 137 for more information) this guide focuses on the 7 areas of prayer used by America Prays. Put this in the hands of all your people who intercede for your city!

You may not be a pastor or a prayer leader, but you are someone who has a burning desire to see your community, maybe even your neighborhood or family, changed by the power of Jesus. This book is for you. We've seen countless individual believers take the concepts in this book, pray them, and begin to see their area changed, little by little, by the power of prayer. Start praying today.

## Our Goal

What's the goal of this book? We want to see cities and communities changed by the power of Jesus Christ. We want to see congregations revived and churches working together in unity to see their cities transformed for the glory of God. We want to see husbands, wives, and singles cry out for God to change what's broken and set things right by his great power and love.

We are seeing God begin to change our city of Austin, Texas through prayer. As you may have heard, there has never been an awakening or revival that did not begin in united prayer. What if God used you to begin a small or large awakening in your family, neighborhood, community, or city? What if people came to Jesus just because you began praying? What if the very God-ordained purpose for your city was released by the prayers of Christians like you in your area? It's happening across America and we believe it can happen in your community.

The history of revival reveals that every move of God began with one or two praying Christians. Each move of God eventually spread to more and more people. But, let's not overlook the one or two who began praying in secret. No one may ever know their names. God continues to change history through simple, unnamed, humble believers who take the time, focus, and faith to ask God to change their city. Someone like you?

The book you hold in your hand, *Praying God's Word over Your City*, is written to inspire, encourage, and equip you to change your world through daily prayer. Jump in, invite your family and friends to pray with you, and ask your church to join in. God has more than you've ever dreamed on the other side of your prayers.

*Section One*

# Pray for Unbelievers to be Saved

# Day 1

## Thankful for My Community

---

*You are the light of the world. A city*
*set on a hill cannot be hidden.*
(Matthew 5:14)

---

Why are you in your city, town, or neighborhood? Were you placed here from birth? Did you come for work? You may have ended up here out of desperation, or felt drawn to this place. This may be a place of joy and anticipation, or you might struggle with boredom from the monotony of being in the same place every day, year after year. What do you love about your community? Take a moment now to thank Jesus for as many gifts as you can appreciate in your place of residence.

*Powerful and wonderful Creator, before the foundation of the earth, you knew and even planned my community. I thank you for the obvious beauty of this place. I even thank you for the obstacles that remind us of our need for you. Thank you for your character (whether hidden in pain or bursting from the seams) that is shown in this city. I'm grateful to be called to live in this community and I'm honored to be empowered by your Holy Spirit to pray as you lead. As I view this place, I see the glory you could reveal in this city and the revival you will bring forth. I ask you to open hearts to the possibility of the transformation you desire in us all and to empower us to believe, pray and work for the glory of your name. Let the gifts you have given our community grow and be used for the healing of our city and the salvation of many.*

*Make _____ the light of the world, a city set on a hill that cannot be hidden. Help us to let our light shine before others, so that they may see our good works and give glory to our Father in heaven.*

## Prayer Points

Reflect on the reason you ended up in your community and thank Jesus for the specific way he placed you in this town.

Think about the gifts your community gives to the world and thank Jesus for the impact your city holds.

What are some of the struggles in your community that God could be using to draw people to himself? Pray that he will use these to reveal his strength in the midst of need and his love in the middle of lack.

What opportunities for Jesus are built into the framework of your community? Ask God to raise up harvesters from all different sectors to shine his light in their realms of influence.

How might God want to use you in your community? Pray for wisdom, strategy and strength to use your gifts and influence to bring revival to your city.

> **The greatest blessing God can send [to your city]
> is Jesus Christ, who will turn people from their
> wickedness, and bring them salvation.**
> — **Intercessors for America**

# Day 2

## Pray for Laborers for the Harvest

---

*Then he said to his disciples, "The harvest is plentiful,
but the laborers are few; therefore pray earnestly to the
Lord of the harvest to send out laborers into his harvest."*
**(Matthew 9:37–38)**

---

The greatest need in our community is not only for the lost to
be saved, but for the saved to become harvesters. How does
this happen? It all begins with prayer. Jesus taught his disciples, and
therefore he is teaching us, to cry out to the Lord of the Harvest asking him to ignite in us the passion and give us the power we desperately need to reach and disciple the lost.

*Lord of the harvest, I cry out to you today in joyful obedience to your
Word. You are full of love for the lost. Give me your passionate desire and
love to see the lost come to know Christ Jesus as Savior and Lord. It gives
me great faith to know that you want me to begin with you, as the source
and power to bring people to salvation. I begin in prayer now, asking for
a fresh filling of the Holy Spirit to empower me to be an effective and loving evangelist in my family, workplace, neighborhood, and community.
Make me a passionate harvester like the disciples were in the book of Acts.*

*Do miracles, convict hearts, and empower believers to make much of Jesus today in my city. Make the name of Jesus first on every believer's heart, and prepare the unbelievers to meet us today as we interact in life. Make reaching out to those without Christ my joy. Remove fear, frustration, and insecurity from my heart and mind. Overwhelm me with your love as I long to be a reconciler of the lost with you. Use me in a way that causes those in need of Christ to look to him as Savior and Lord. Jesus, convince me and fellow believers that this is the greatest work of the church—to seek and save the lost as you did when you walked the earth. Thank you for affirming that you are both for me and with me as I step out in faith today to be a harvester. I thank you in advance that you are making me a fruitful and faithful witness for Christ today. In Jesus' name, Amen.*

## Prayer Points

Ask for forgiveness for letting fear and the world stifle your evangelistic fervor.

Seek God for a fresh filling of the Holy Spirit today to empower you with boldness.

Rejoice that God is for you and with you in this mission.

Intercede for family members, neighbors, and fellow church members to be mobilized as harvesters.

Pray specifically for lost family, friends, work associates, and neighbors. Ask that you can be a clear and loving witness for Jesus Christ as soon as possible.

> **The missionary church is a praying church. The history of missions is a history of prayer. Everything vital to the success of the world's evangelization hinges on prayer.**
> **— John Mott**

# *Day 3*

༄

# Cry Out for a Heart to
# see the Lost Saved

*Brothers, my heart's desire and prayer to*
*God for them is that they may be saved.*
**(Romans 10:1)**

The prayer of World Vision's founder, Bob Pierce, has been rightfully and often repeated: "Let my heart be broken with the things that break the heart of God."

Injustice, illness, poverty, and devastation are in the news and on our minds every day. There are many reasons to grieve for ourselves and others. We know that Jesus' heart is tender to all the burdens we bear, but nothing moves his heart like the lostness that is found in a soul that is separated from him. Our eyes quickly move to the physical depravity of the world and somehow skip naively over the only permanent loss in all of eternity.

Every problem that steals our sleep and wrestles peace from our minds is temporary. Someday, there will be no more sickness, violence, hatred or lack. Everything will be made right in the eternal kingdom of God. All will be well for those who are forever in the heart and arms of Jesus, but for those who have not given their lives to Jesus, all will be lost. To live and die without Christ is to face the only permanent loss known to man.

Do we realize that when Jesus cried over Jerusalem, his heart was wrenched because he knew that without his gift of salvation, they had no hope? Do we understand that every face we see in the grocery store, every footstep we hear coming down the hall, and every life we encounter has an eternal destiny that will either lead to eternity with Jesus or a never-ending separation from his life and love?

God's greatest desire is that all the world would know his Son and be found safe for eternity in him. Let's ask Jesus to put his heart of compassion within us and to move our hearts to pray and work for the salvation of many.

*Gracious heavenly Father, thank you for sending Jesus to die on the cross for my sins and the sins of the world. I repent for my lack of compassion and urgency to see the lost saved. Forgive me for apathy and short-sightedness. Cleanse me of all selfishness and arrogance. I ask you, Father, to change my heart and make it break for what breaks your heart. I ask you to give me a heart of compassion and a will to witness in every way possible. Holy Spirit, fill me with your presence and anoint me with your words so that I may witness passionately and continually for you. Give me a heart to pray and not give up until your will is done in bringing many to righteousness.*

## Prayer Points

Take a moment and ask the Holy Spirit to show you happenings, activities and attitudes in your city that break his heart. Ask God to give you his compassion for people who are affected by the sin and lostness of your community.

Ask Jesus to show you where you have been apathetic and negligent in praying for and witnessing to the lost in your community. Repent of specific areas and situations where you have chosen to ignore the call to share him with others

Submit your heart and mind to the Holy Spirit and allow him to give you a list of people for whom you will pray and with whom you will share.

Take the list you have made and commit to pray for them daily and to look for opportunities to share the love of God with them.

**Break my heart for what breaks yours;**
**Everything I am for your kingdom's cause.**

— "Hosanna" (Hillsong)

# Day 4

❧

# Ask for All to Come
to Repentance

---

*The Lord is not slow to fulfill his promise as some count*
*slowness, but is patient toward you, not wishing that*
*any should perish, but that all should reach repentance.*
**(2 Peter 3:9)**

---

$A$*ll* is a huge word. Think about that. The Scriptures call us to
pray and witness to all people. No one is beyond the grace of
God as long as they live. This should drive our prayers. We have a
Father who doesn't want any to perish, but *all* to come to repentance.
May we have this same heart. May our prayers reflect this one passion. May our lives overflow with this heart of love for all people,
even today.

*Lord, I ask today, in keeping with your Word, that I would have*
*an indiscriminate heart, a heart of love for all people—no matter what*
*race or creed. May the love of Jesus flow through me to all people, know-*
*ing it's your desire that all people come to repentance. This is why your*
*people, including me, must share the gospel with all people. Help me*
*with the "all." Thank you for your love and power that can transform*
*even the worst of sinners, and the religious sinner who is hiding behind*

*his boisterous ways to cover a lost heart. May patience be my attitude as I consistently love and share you with those difficult to reach. Make me like you, not wanting any to perish but all to come to repentance. Repentance is a great gift you give to humans. I pray I will have the privilege of seeing people turn to you today. Do it, Lord! Use my witness and my life to reach out to the "all" whom you love and the "all" for whom you are delaying your return to see reached. Cause people to repent today, my Lord. We joyfully receive your mercy. Cause your saints to be effective in reaching the lost today.*

*In Jesus' name, Amen.*

## Prayer Points

Seek God's forgiveness for any and all distinctions you've made between those who seem to be reachable for Christ and those who do not.

Believe that Father God will give you his heart of love equally for all.

Ask today to see the lost repent and turn to Christ in saving faith.

Receive from God a fresh empowerment to display the fruit of the Spirit, including patience, as you interact with those far from God.

Pray specifically for those in your life who are hard to reach. Pray they will come to repentance.

> **Repentance is not a few hot tears at the penitent form. It is not emotion or remorse or reformation. Repentance is a change of mind about God, about sin, and about hell!**
>
> **—Leonard Ravenhill**

*Day 5*

⁓

# Seek God to Remove the Blinders from the Eyes of Unbelievers

---

*In their case the god of this world has blinded the minds of the unbelievers, to keep them from seeing the light of the gospel of the glory of Christ, who is the image of God. For what we proclaim is not ourselves, but Jesus Christ as Lord, with ourselves as your servants for Jesus' sake. For God, who said, "Let light shine out of darkness," has shone in our hearts to give the light of the knowledge of the glory of God in the face of Jesus Christ.*
**(2 Corinthians 4:4–6)**

---

The spiritual warfare for the souls of men and women, boys and girls, is raging before our very eyes. May we not be ignorant of the enemy's schemes to deceive and destroy the lives of those we seek to reach for Christ. Being aware of the spiritual forces that are waging war all around us is half the battle. The other half is diligently fighting the good fight through prayer and evangelism. Let's seek God for his infinite power to see the lost freed to see the glory of Jesus.

*Father, today I seek your face, asking that you would awaken me to the spiritual war that rages all around me. Focus me on the greater power, influence, and victory that is already won through Jesus Christ my Lord. Free me not only to recognize the spiritual battles, but to be mobilized in prevailing prayer and victorious outreach toward those in the clutches of Satan's lies and deception. Today, Father, I cry out for those I love and for those in my neighborhood and workplace to be freed from the blinders that our ancient foe has used to keep them trapped in a lost state of hell-bound ignorance. Use me and your people to proclaim Jesus Christ today. Forgive me for proclaiming my thoughts and my ways. Remove my self-centered focus as I lift up the death, burial, and resurrection of Jesus Christ. May Jesus remain front and center in my witnessing today. Open the eyes of the lost to see the glory of God in the face of Christ. Jesus, you asked that we would see your glory. Today, I ask that you answer that prayer by removing blinders of deception that plague those with whom I interact on a daily basis. Show your glory today by freeing the lost from a spiritual blindness that can only be healed by you. Show them the joy, beauty, power, awe, and love that are in you and you alone!*

## Prayer Points

Thank God that he is greater than all, including all the forces of the enemy.

Ask God to remove the spiritual blinders for specific people in your world.

Seek God for open doors to share the gospel, which has the power to deliver.

Intercede for believers to preach Christ, not ourselves.

Trust God that he will reveal his glory to the lost today.

I find myself praying more and more, Lord, fill our church with a passion to open the eyes of the blind. Fill us with a passion to do what God uses to bring about the new birth.

— John Piper

# Day 6

⟳

# Intercede for the Gospel to Be Proclaimed World-Wide

*And this gospel of the kingdom will be proclaimed throughout the whole world as a testimony to all nations, and then the end will come.*

(Matthew 24:14)

The gospel rings out from church bells in ancient villages, is quietly sung under the cover of darkness in hidden woods, is raucously celebrated in crowded and boisterous urban amphitheaters and is happily proclaimed by dancing worshipers in tribal communities. All over the world, the name of Jesus is celebrated—or so we hope. It brings us joy to hear songs of praise in many languages, but it also rips our hearts wide open to realize that there are still many who've yet to hear, understand, and follow the ONE who holds all that is needed by this lost and lonely world. As violence tears through our streets and evil threatens to separate even the closest of friends, we long to see the return of Jesus. We know, however, that if our Savior were to come today, many would die without the eternal hope of knowing him forever. This is not his heart, and because of our love for him, it is not our desire either. Let's pray for the name of Jesus to be known, loved and followed all over the world. Let's ask for the strength, the means, and the heart to take his gospel to each listening ear in every beautiful language.

*All-loving Father, thank you for making such a beautifully diverse world. We honor your creativity in developing various languages, cultures, and so many gorgeous expressions of your image. You were right to put us in the lands of your choosing, and wise to ordain the places of our habitation. We know that your heart is not willing that any should live and die without an opportunity to know you and live for you. We ask that you take your message to those who've not yet heard your name. Please send evangelists of love and truth to show them the glory you have prepared for all who choose you and allow missionaries the privilege of leading them into a relationship with your own dear Son. Raise up leaders in every land to know you and make you known. Give those of us in lands who are rich with your name and your Word the heart and the opportunity to share from the wealth of our resources so that many may know and grow in you. Draw us out of our apathy. Rescue us from our fear. Equip us with all that we need to make you known to these dear ones for whom you died. Prepare the entire world for your coming by making your name known. Send us across the ocean, around the corner and even into the next room to share your story of love and salvation. Use us in any way you choose to proclaim your gospel all over the world for the glory of your name.*

## Prayer Points

Pray for a heart to love and share Jesus with the lost.

Pray for a change in priorities of time and wealth that would enable us to sacrificially give so that the name of Jesus will be known.

Pray for God-ordained opportunities to go to every man, woman and child with the message of Jesus.

Pray for hearts, civilizations and cultures to be prepared to hear and receive Jesus.

> **We have all eternity to celebrate the victories, but only a few hours before sunset to win them.**
>
> — Amy Carmichael

*Section Two*

# Pray for a National Spiritual Awakening

# Day 7

❧

# Pray for Personal and Corporate Revival

*When I shut up the heavens so that there is no
rain, or command the locust to devour the land,
or send pestilence among my people, if my people
who are called by my name humble themselves,
and pray and seek my face and turn from their
wicked ways, then I will hear from heaven and
will forgive their sin and heal their land.*
(2 Chronicles 7:13–14)

God places the responsibility for revival upon his children. He gives us a clear and concise strategy to compel us to remedy tragedies in our society and to be a part of seeing true and lasting revival in our land. Some have claimed this promise is only for Israel, but they are gravely mistaken. The Bible says all the promises of God are yes for us in Christ! Paul, inspired by the Holy Spirit, was referring to the Old Testament promises. They are ours to claim and embrace as we trust God for a new work of grace in our communities.

*Father, I pray today, in keeping with your ancient remedy for the ills of society and your benevolent promise for a healed land, that you would send revival, and start with me! Do a work of grace inside me that causes me to humble myself, pray, seek your face, and turn from my wicked ways. I need a revived heart and life more than anyone else. Gracious Father, as you revive me, would you revive my family as well? Cause passion for Jesus to be the norm in our family line. Let no one go to hell who is a part of my family.*

*May this revival spread to my church! Cause holy fire for you and your name to consume our church family. May this love for Jesus overflow from my church and impact my neighborhood and the neighborhoods around our church families. May this revival that we long for transform our city! May our community experience everything Jesus died and rose again to do here. May our city impact our state. Please revive our state, making each city a place where Jesus is treasured and exalted. May our state be a champion for revival in our nation. May every part of our country blaze with holy zeal for the Lord. And, may our nation be a tool in your hand to spread a hunger and thirst for Jesus to the nations of the world. Father, let it begin with me, but let it not end there. I ask that the knowledge of God would cover the earth like water the sea. Let me see this in my lifetime!*

*In Jesus' name, Amen.*

## Prayer Points

Seek Jesus for a personal revival in keeping with 2 Chronicles 7:14.

Intercede for believing family members to be set ablaze for Christ.

Ask God to send revival to your local church.

Request from God to send a revival that would impact your neighborhood.

Believe God for the church in your state to be ignited with Holy fire for God.

Cry out for God to send a historic awakening to your nation.

Plead with God to send revival to specific nations he puts on your heart.

**Second Chronicles 7:14 is revival on God's terms.**

**— Dr. Walter Kiser, Jr.**

# Day 8

## Plead for Restoration of our Devastated Cities

*O my God, incline your ear and hear. Open your eyes and see our desolations, and the city that is called by your name. For we do not present our pleas before you because of our righteousness, but because of your great mercy. O Lord, hear; O Lord, forgive. O Lord, pay attention and act. Delay not, for your own sake, O my God, because your city and your people are called by your name."*
**(Daniel 9:18–19)**

God determined the exact families that we were born into and the specific locations that we live so that we might seek God and help others know him (Acts 17:26). In other words, we have been appointed to our city or community by God to work for the blessing of the city (Jeremiah 29:7). Devastated cities or communities are healed and restored by healed and restored people (Isaiah 61:4). The transformation of a city begins in private prayer, but must grow into a united cry resulting in unified labor for a move of God that turns the city upside down. Let's contend for this!

*Father God, I plead for you to hear and answer this request, in keeping with your Word, that you would open the eyes of your church to the devastations in our community. May we see the evil as you see it. May we hate the evil as you hate it. I cry out today, because you have placed me in my city, for mercy for my community. Without your mercy, we will be condemned to utter destruction. Let our individual cries for a changed community morph into a united cry for your kingdom to come, and your will to be done in our area today. I ask that the restoration of our devastated city would begin with a mighty movement of prayer across denominational lines, all for the glory of Jesus. I plead with you to raise up prayer warriors and Spirit-empowered laborers to work together to preach the gospel, bring justice, build relationships, fight poverty, establish righteousness, and see our community become all you died to make us to be. Here am I, send me.*

## Prayer Points

Ask God to burden your heart to pray for your community to be transformed.

Seek God for a unified prayer movement to be established in your area.

Request that God-empowered workers will be mobilized to see the lost saved, and your city healed.

Pray that the unique gifting of your city will be used to bring the utmost glory to Jesus.

**The man who mobilizes the Christian church
to pray will make the greatest contribution
to world evangelization in history.**

**— Andrew Murray**

# Day 9

Cry Out for the Lost to Be
Saved in Large Numbers

---

*Now when they heard this they were cut to the heart,*
*and said to Peter and the rest of the apostles, "Brothers,*
*what shall we do?" And Peter said to them, "Repent and*
*be baptized every one of you in the name of Jesus Christ*
*for the forgiveness of your sins, and you will receive the*
*gift of the Holy Spirit. For the promise is for you and for*
*your children and for all who are far off, everyone whom*
*the Lord our God calls to himself." And with many other*
*words he bore witness and continued to exhort them,*
*saying, "Save yourselves from this crooked generation."*
*So those who received his word were baptized, and*
*there were added that day about three thousand souls.*
(Acts 2:37–41)

---

Every Sunday in America some 400,000 congregations gather and
the good news of Jesus Christ is preached. In your community,
churches gather. What would happen if every pastor had a prayer
team that prayed while the preacher preached? Charles Spurgeon
said the power of his sermons were attributed to the several hundred

deacons who prayed in the church basement while he preached the word of God powerfully. Let's cry out today for those who preach the gospel to many people in your church and community, whether they be pastors or rank and file believers.

*Father, I cry out today for the Word to go forth in the power I read about in the book of Acts. May conviction come with such power that those who hear it ask, "What must I do to be saved?" I pray for my pastor and for area pastors to raise up a mighty praying people who pray while the preacher preaches. Let me be one of these prayer warriors. I ask for all believers to be empowered to share Jesus boldly and to see the lost repent, be saved, and baptized.*

*Holy Spirit, fill your people to overflowing. May we be salt and light. May the salt get out of the salt shaker and flow into the world. Use me today to share Jesus clearly with one person. I pray now that he or she will be receptive to hear your Word. I ask that this year our community would see a greater number of people saved and discipled than we've seen in our history. Do a fresh, new, Holy Spirit-empowered work. Bring a great awakening to our community so that we can have a "before and after" perspective of your mighty work. We are eager to see a powerful move of God. Use me today. In Jesus' name, Amen.*

## Prayer Points

Pray for churches and pastors (by name) to preach powerfully the gospel of Jesus Christ.

Ask God for specific believers to be mighty evangelists.

Seek God for a great awakening in your community.

**If the Lord tarries and there is no revival of pure
Christianity, then the next span of years will
be the worst history has ever recorded.**

**— Leonard Ravenhill**

# Day 10

## Ask God to Make Revivalists Out of the Lost

*Many Samaritans from that town believed in him because of the woman's testimony, "He told me all that I ever did." So, when the Samaritans came to him, they asked him to stay with them, and he stayed there two days. And many more believed because of his word. They said to the woman, "It is no longer because of what you said that we believe, for we have heard for ourselves, and we know that this is indeed the Savior of the world."*

**(John 4:39–42)**

It started with an unplanned meeting between two painfully segregated strangers. Many would have said that these two should have never spoken a sentence to one another, this deeply religious Jew and a woman of questionable character and despised race. When their conversation turned to the life-changing reality of God's miraculous provision for this lost and lonely Samaritan woman, her eyes were not only opened but her heart was set free to live the truth of this gospel and to offer it to anyone who would listen. As she recounted the story, the people of her village were intrigued and as they met the man Jesus, they were persuaded to believe.

Think about those in your city who have been marginalized by society or who, by their own wayward choices, have been left hopeless and destitute. Remember those whose worldly ways make them seem like the least likely candidates to be chosen by God to spread his message. Could they be the very souls Jesus wants to use to usher in revival? Could the story of their changed lives and the example of their salvation stoke the fires that could ignite hope and faith? Let's pray that, once again, Jesus will use unexpected evangelists to bring revival and restoration to our cities.

*Jesus, Living Water for all thirsty souls, we ask that you draw the hurting and weary of our city into a life-changing encounter with you. We ask you to take those bent on destruction and make them builders of your kingdom. We pray that you would soften hard hearts and allow them to hear your tender voice. We pray for our own hearts to be softened toward all who need you. Forgive us for judging them wrongly for we know that we too are in constant need of your grace. Empower and send us to share your story and to offer your gift of salvation to many. Give us hearts to love and faith to believe that you can transform sinners into mighty revivalists for the glory of your name. Cause us to pray, work, and never give up so that we may see these dear ones for whom you died become the vessels of grace through whom you will live. Turn everything the enemy of their souls has meant for evil into good for the saving of many. We thank you for giving us the privilege of praying for these whom you love and ask you to fill us with your compassion, your hope and your encouragement as we believe for the work of revival you will do in and through them.*

## Prayer Points

Repent for any and every way you have overlooked, judged, or ignored the lost in your community.

Ask Jesus to give you his perspective and his heart for what he wants to do through these dear ones.

Pray for groups in your city whom you have considered to be unlikely evangelists (the homeless, those of different religions, the very rich or the very poor). Ask the Holy Spirit to draw them to himself.

Pray for specific individuals in your sphere of influence who need to come to a saving knowledge of Jesus. Ask the Holy Spirit to guide you as you pray for them.

Pray for ministries who are reaching out to specific groups (college ministers, ministries to immigrants, outreaches to the poor).

> **God sometimes uses very weak and unlikely instruments for beginning and carrying on a good work. Our Savior, by teaching one poor woman, spread knowledge to a whole town.**
>
> **— Matthew Henry**

## Day 11

*Intercede for Mercy Over Wrath*

---

*O Lord, I have heard the report of you, and your work, O Lord, do I fear. In the midst of the years revive it; in the midst of the years make it known; in wrath remember mercy.*
(Habakkuk 3:2)

---

When Adam and Eve disobeyed in the garden, God knew that after he disciplined them, he would prepare a way for them to once again walk with him. As he poured forth torrential floods to cleanse the earth of sin, the eternal Savior was preparing an ark to bring those who would follow him to safety. While their rebellion caused God to unleash a forty-year punishment on the Israelites, they also lived out his mercy as the Red Sea parted to let them cross to the land of promise. Our God has always been just, but his mercy has never faltered. The same God who allows consequences of sin to disrupt our lives, has prepared an inexhaustible answer for all who will choose him. His mercy triumphs over judgment (Amos 7:9). He is ready and waiting to offer his incomprehensible, never-failing mercy to our communities. Let's invite him to heal our land through his mercy.

*Merciful Father, we thank you that your mercies are new every morning and that you always long to show compassion to us. We ask you to remember the covenant you have made with us through your own Son and plead with you to pour mercy over us today. Forgive us for every way we have incurred and do rightly deserve your wrath. We repent of the evil we have done and the wrong we have permitted in our community. We know that we have sinned against your holy nature as we have lived unjustly and refused to show your love to a hurt and dying world. We ask you to pour waves of grace over our lives that would run through the streets of our city. Please use us to show your grace to those whom you love. Show us how to offer and give your mercy to those who need it most. We know that we deserve judgment, and thank you that through the cross, you have provided the payment for our sins. We receive your mercy and we covenant with you to show it to others today. Bring a revival of grace and mercy to our community, dear Lord, and initiate it with us.*

## Prayer Points

Ask for forgiveness for the sins that have brought about our need for judgment (Be specific as you remember your sins and the sins of your community).

Repent of every way you have failed to show God's mercy to those who need it most—whether it be through wrong actions or selfish apathy.

Ask Jesus to pour his mercy over your city today.

Ask the Holy Spirit to guide you to find and do acts of mercy in your community today.

Commit to receiving and giving the mercy of Jesus today.

God's mercy is his goodness toward those in distress,
his grace is his goodness toward those who deserve only
punishment, and his patience is his goodness toward
those who continue to sin over a period of time.

— Wayne A. Grudem

# Day 12

## Pray for Revival

*Will you not revive us again, that your
people may rejoice in you?*
**(Psalm 85:6)**

We often pray for revival as we see the deadness in the church and the devastation in our community, but do we long for it so that our cities can be filled with rejoicing? It has been said that God is the happiest being in the universe and yet, somehow, we tend to see only his desire for reverence, holiness and repentance. Can we believe that the God who made us wants to fill our hearts and our neighborhoods with joy? As we experience the resurrection of our spirits, we will also know the JOY that comes from him.

Many of us have come to believe that our holiness should cause us to override and even shun the need to experience an emotional connection with our heavenly Father, but John 15 assures us that if we keep his commandments and abide in his love, our joy will be full. Many powerful manifestations will come from the revival we await and one of the most pleasant will be rejoicing as we see God's mighty work. Let's continue to fiercely contend for revival and let's excitedly anticipate the JOY that it will bring.

*Joyful Father, we rejoice in you and thank you that your heart is to always connect with us. We praise you for giving us the ability to enjoy your presence and the many ways you bless us. We ask you to bring revival so we may rejoice in you and in the works of your joyful hands. You know that the burdens we carry are heavy and that there is much to discourage us. Would you fill us with your Holy Spirit, today, so we may rejoice in you and see beyond the distractions that steal our joy? We ask you to allow us to see the hidden work of grace you are doing in our community so we may open our hearts and mouths in praise to you. We joyfully anticipate the revival that is coming and thank you for allowing us to rejoice in you.*

## Prayer Points

Ask the Holy Spirit to give you the strength to continually abide in him and to raise up many in your community who are living in close relationship with him.

Pray for people in your city who are working diligently for Jesus that they may be overwhelmed with joy in their ministry.

Ask the Lord to show you areas of sin, apathy and pain that you need to surrender to him, so he may fill you with his joy.

Pray that the joy of the Lord will be your strength today as you believe for revival.

Ask Jesus to give you eyes to see the work that he is already doing toward revival in your city.

**Revival is falling in love with Jesus all over again.**

— Vance Havner

*Section Three*

# Pray for the Unity
of the Church

# Day 13

## Cry Out for God to Make Us One

*I do not ask for these only, but also for those who will believe in me through their word, that they may all be one, just as you, Father, are in me, and I in you, that they also may be in us, so that the world may believe that you have sent me. The glory that you have given me I have given to them, that they may be one even as we are one, I in them and you in me, that they may become perfectly one, so that the world may know that you sent me and loved them even as you loved me.*
(John 17:20–23)

How can we pray better than our Lord Jesus prayed? We cannot. But we can agree with his prayer through our own prayers and with our very lives. The battle for true oneness must overcome the barriers of race, geographical distance, cultural differences, socioeconomic distinctions, and other untold enemies of God-based unity. We know God is greater. Jesus' prayer in John 17 is being answered now and will be fully answered in the days to come. We are one in Christ, but our realized oneness is still being made known. Strictly

speaking, we are already one. Practically speaking, we must see many
walls removed to be able to fully celebrate this blood-bought reality
purchased by Jesus Christ. This is a battle worth waging, for our
unity brings our heavenly Father magnificent praise and glory.

*Father God, I cry out to you today in keeping with your Son Jesus
Christ's prayer: Make us one, even as you and he are one. Magnify your
unmatched majesty by shattering ancient and demonic walls that divide
your people. I know Jesus died to remove the wall of hostility between
members of the body of Christ. Stop our fighting. Heal our wounds.
Let forgiveness be given. May hearts be aligned. As you have filled your
people with your very own Spirit, let the Holy Spirit bring a unity and
peace to the people of God that has not been seen in generations. Let
our love for one another be a sign and a wonder on the earth. I ask that
your glory would radiate through the beautiful symmetry of your saved
ones working together, eating together, praying together, and honoring
one another. My Lord, I long to see such a clear and powerful unity that
even the world itself will take notice of the spectacle of your church living and loving as the healthiest family, loving and serving in your power
and presence. May our unity be the strongest evangelistic tool we have
and may our deference for one another cause the world to look at our
wonderful Savior Jesus Christ. Cause our love for one another to be so
tenacious, unselfish, and tender that the lost will know, by virtue of this
miracle, that a Source of love exists that is out of this world. I ask that
the love, unity, and oneness of your people would make you both famous
and followed in our community. In Jesus' name, Amen.*

## Prayer Points

Pray for a work of oneness in your community that is rooted in the
Father and Son's complete unity.

Cry out for healing of old and new divisions between Christians and
congregations in your area.

Ask God to raise up pastors, prayer warriors, and Christians of all types to forge a practical and visible unity between congregations in your town or city.

Intercede for the body of Christ to bring God great glory through forgiveness, working together, and honoring one another above ourselves.

Plead with God for the demonic oppression ruling your area to be driven out as the people of God experience the blood-bought oneness that Jesus purchased through his death, burial, resurrection, and outpouring of the Spirit.

> **Believers are never told to become one; we already are one and are expected to act like it.**
>
> — Joni Eareckson Tada

*Day 14*

⁕

# Plead for Jesus to Bring a Unity that Causes His Blessing to Cover Our City

---

*Behold, how good and pleasant it is*
  *when brothers dwell in unity!*
*It is like the precious oil on the head,*
  *running down on the beard,*
*on the beard of Aaron,*
  *running down on the collar of his robes!*
*It is like the dew of Hermon,*
  *which falls on the mountains of Zion!*
*For there the LORD has commanded the blessing,*
  *life forevermore.*

**(Psalm 133)**

---

Can you imagine what it would be like for your entire community to be under a canopy of God's blessing? It's hard to imagine; isn't it? I read the incredible firsthand account of the 1949–1952 Hebrides Revival. For three years, God's tangible presence was known throughout the island of Lewis. Simply put, virtually all the people were either experiencing the conviction of the Lord or the joy of the Lord. What would happen if God commanded a blessing on our unity that resulted in the tangible presence of the Holy Spirit resting upon our communities? Let's ask!

*Lord Jesus, today I come pleading with you for a work of grace upon our community. I see the devastating results of the curse of sin and death. My city needs to see the blessing of God's Spirit resting over our area as a tent over a family. Your Word promises a commanded blessing on brothers and sisters as we walk in unity. We need a sovereign breakthrough. Break off our petty divisions. Unearth our fallow ground. Resurrect our broken unity. Send forth your power and might to heal our land. You are our living hope! Bring unprecedented unity in my life, family, neighborhood, church, city, state, nation, and world. Root this work in your transforming work on the cross. Let the oil of the Holy Spirit drip down over your Body in our area. Make us a beautiful reflection of a blessed land. Be exalted here. Humble us in the lifting up of your mighty name. Use me as an ambassador of unity. I ask for a work of peace and healing to be wrought today in our town. We need you. We are desperate for what only you can do! We trust you today for this work of love in our community. In Jesus' name, Amen.*

## Prayer Points

Ask that visible unity would emerge in your community through prayer, compassion, worship, etc.

Repent over historic divisions that have taken root in your city between races, groups, churches, family, and friends.

Intercede for churches to experience true, biblical unity.

Seek God for an area-wide blessing of unity and a canopy of God's presence in your town.

And an awareness of God gripped the community such as hadn't been known for over 100 years. An awareness of God—that's revival, that's revival.

— Duncan Campbell

# Day 15

~~~

# Ask God to Empower Us to Love One Another

*By this all people will know that you are my disciples, if you have love for one another.*
**(John 13:35)**

A quick scroll through social media will tell you that, of all the things we Christians portray, loving one another is not at the top of the list. It is often not on any list of our attributes at all! This is heartbreaking to Jesus and devastating to our lives. Jesus knew that only through our unity would his relationship with the Father and the Holy Spirit be truly exhibited. He knew that without unity, we would be weak, fearful and overwhelmed by loneliness. The enemy of our souls also knows that if he can divide us, he can conquer our most powerful evangelistic plans and cause us to fail to live out our most sincere prayers. Loving one another as Christ loved the church, sacrificially, generously and humbly, can never be done on our own. Our fearful and self-centered natures must be overcome and empowered by the strength of the Holy Spirit living in us. When he moves through us, not only can mountains be moved, but stony hearts can be softened and molded to be full of his transforming love. Let's ask the Holy Spirit to make us living, breathing, and loving agents of change in our communities so many may know and live in his love. *Jesus, Lover of our souls, we are eternally grateful for the way you have loved us! You have given, served and healed our souls. You have called us your very own and have loved us unconditionally in spite of our many failures. We repent of every way we have been ruled by our own selfishness. Forgive us for making our agenda, our opinions and our preferences more important than your call to love one another. Cleanse us of the apathy and self-protectiveness that hinder our love for one another. Give us your heart and allow us to see our brothers and sisters through your eyes of compassion and understanding. Make us one as you and the Father are one. We ask you to make the love we have for one another an irresistible invitation to the world to come into your loving and welcoming family. We cannot do this on our own. We humble ourselves in your presence and ask you to fill us with your Holy Spirit so we may love as you love. Overwhelm us with your compassion today and use our lives to share your heart with a hurting world who needs the acceptance and healing that only come through you. We love you, Jesus, and want to love your children. Thank you that you long to answer this prayer and that you are remaking us to be your agents of love.*

## Prayer Points

Ask Jesus to bring to mind the ways you have lived selfishly and without love. Take a moment to repent for as many as come to mind.

Ask the Holy Spirit to fill you with his love and to empower you to see your brothers and sisters in Christ through his eyes of compassion.

Let the heavenly Father show you whom you need to forgive for any way they have failed to love you. Surrender your hurt to Jesus and forgive them now.

Prayerfully, make a list of anyone Jesus leads you to show tangible love to today. We are told to do good to everyone, especially

to those in the household of faith (Galatians 6:10). Ask the Holy
Spirit to give you creative ideas and empowerment to put this love
into action.

> Do not waste time bothering whether you "love" your
> neighbor; act as if you did. As soon as we do this we find
> one of the great secrets. When you are behaving as if you
> loved someone, you will presently come to love him.
>
> — C. S. Lewis

# Day 16

## Request of God That We May Live as One People Before the Throne of God

---

*After this I looked, and behold, a great multitude that no one could number, from every nation, from all tribes and peoples and languages, standing before the throne and before the Lamb, clothed in white robes, with palm branches in their hands.*
**(Revelation 7:9)**

---

The beauty and majesty as described in heaven will be astounding. Every color and each texture will emanate the glory of God. Every sound and rhythm will carry the message of his wonder, but none will show forth his glory more brilliantly than the faces of those he has redeemed. Every tribe and every nation will be before the throne worshiping and thanking Jesus for his gift of eternal life. How wonderful it will be to see each skin tone and all of the languages joining together in praise.

The sad reality is that today we are separated not merely by distance and language, but by a large chasm of misunderstanding, suspicion and apathy. The enemy of our souls has worked a deception on our hearts and minds to keep us from experiencing the glory of God together. He has whispered lies and we have believed that we are more different than we are the same. We have allowed hurt and ignorance to lead us into grave sin and have marred the image of Christ by our hatred and our indifference.

Jesus has a better plan. Jesus has made a better way for us to live and love as one. What miracle of grace would the world behold if we were united as one people under Jesus? Let's ask him to free us of our sin and unite us so we may worship together and display his glory to a world who desperately needs to know him.

*Powerful and wise Father, we thank you that in your wisdom you created us with a variety of beautiful distinctions and lovingly placed us all over the world. We are grateful for each language and all of the cultures that you envisioned. Help us, Jesus, to enjoy the gifts of culture and language and to use them to glorify you. Show us how to come together for the glory of your name and the salvation of many. Please forgive us for our selfishness and the many ways we have exalted our own preferences and backgrounds above your plan to unite us in you. Give us humble and forgiving hearts so we may offer the grace we've been given to all who would hurt and offend us.*

*We know that it is through our unity that many will see and be drawn into your loving arms. Show us how to creatively and faithfully find ways to unite as one body with one purpose and vision to make you known all over the world. We exalt you as Creator, Lord and Savior and commit to making your name famous and followed. We pray that your name will be known and received among unreached people and that you will send us boldly and compassionately to everyone's world with your gospel. Equip us with all that we need to bring to you the reward of your sacrifice.*

## Prayer Points

Envision the people mentioned in Revelation 7:9 and thank Jesus for bringing them to his throne of grace.

Think of a people group around the world and pray for their salvation and discipleship.

Ask God to bring to mind a people group in your own community that needs to be touched by his gospel. Pray for workers to be sent to them and for their hearts to be readied to receive the message of salvation. Ask Jesus what he would have you do for these people

Ask the Holy Spirit to show you a group you have not loved. Repent and ask him to give you his heart to love them.

**Can you sense the heartbreak of God for the multitudes of lost people who have yet to know of his grace?**

**— Living the Way Ministries**

# Day 17

## Seek God to Enable us to Maintain the Unity of the Spirit

---

*I therefore, a prisoner for the Lord, urge you to walk
in a manner worthy of the calling to which you have
been called, with all humility and gentleness, with
patience, bearing with one another in love, eager to
maintain the unity of the Spirit in the bond of peace.
There is one body and one Spirit—just as you were
called to the one hope that belongs to your call—one
Lord, one faith, one baptism, one God and Father
of all, who is over all and through all and in all.*
(Ephesians 4:1–6)

---

To walk in a manner worthy of the Lord is to walk unlike the
world, and even unlike much of the church world. The high
calling upon us is to walk in humility, gentleness, patience, and love.
These are the building blocks of true, Jesus-glorifying unity. Many
of us have been raised in a culture of independence, in families with
deep brokenness, and live where division is commonplace. Now we

are born into a kingdom, a family, where unity is the atmosphere and grace and love are the fuel for this blood-bought oneness in Jesus Christ. Let's contend for this unity. Seek God for our lives, families, churches, and communities to display the unity he calls for and empowers us to enjoy.

*Father God, I seek you today with my whole heart for your people in my community to walk in a manner worthy of our calling. Cause us to overflow with love, patience, gentleness, and humility. I ask that our Jesus communities and families would shine forth in contrast to this world, a symmetrical and consistent love expressed in deep and lasting unity. Today, enable me and your people to bear with one another. Open our eyes to see that, together, we are one body, and that each one of your people is joined together in this one body that we might live and work in complete agreement. Praise you that your one Spirit has filled all your people. Your Spirit makes us one. We all carry and are filled with the same unifying Holy Spirit. Today, may your Spirit overflow in your people, shining forth the one hope that belongs to us all. May your hope in us be shared clearly and purely with the watching world. Our unity rests in our one Lord, one faith, and one baptism. There is so much more that unifies us than divides us. Manifest your Spirit of unity in your church in our community this day. In Jesus' name, Amen.*

## Prayer Points

Seek God for a fresh work of love, humility, and gentleness to invade and consume his people.

Repent for the ways you have not walked in a manner worthy of your calling, especially in the areas of love and unity.

Pray that pastors, leaders, and Christians will know and understand there is only one body, but many congregations. Ask that a visible unity of the one church would be displayed in your community.

Ask the Holy Spirit to fill your congregation, and the area congregations, in a visible and unifying way.

Contend for a bright display of our seven-fold unity of one Body, one Lord, one Hope, one Baptism, one Spirit, one Faith, and one God and Father over all.

> **Many Scripture passages could be called to witness that love is the real key to Christian unity. In the spirit of true humility, compassion, consideration, and unselfishness, we are to approach our problems, our work, and even our differences.**
>
> — Billy Graham

## Day 18

⌒

# Intercede for the Body
# of Christ to Celebrate
# Our Differences

———

*For as in one body we have many members, and*
*the members do not all have the same function,*
*so we, though many, are one body in Christ,*
*and individually members one of another.*
**(Romans 12:4–5)**

———

I sat spellbound as I watched a brother powerfully defend our faith from beginning to end with facts, figures and even scientific data. How could anyone take the heart-piercing beauty of Jesus' loving gospel and so eloquently and convincingly explain it in a way that would capture the mind of an intellectual? I certainly don't share that kind of intellectual prowess.

With the same heart and a different gifting, my sister Susan pours a cup of coffee for each person at church as if she were serving Christ himself. Her gifts of hospitality and service have prepared many fearful and hesitant souls to receive the message of Jesus.

How beautiful are the gifts of the Spirit as displayed through his children! What a treasure we experience every time one of our clay vessels pours forth God's love in the distinct and personal offering we are privileged to give. The family of God is beautiful! She is black, white, brown, yellow, red—all shades of flesh imaginable. She votes Republican, Democrat, independent—and sometimes refrains from voting at all. She is active and peaceful, boisterous and calm. The body of Christ is alive, diverse and gifted. The unified church is beautifully diverse and eternally powerful. We are, together, *his* Body, completely different and miraculously united in *him*. We are one in Jesus.

Instead of quibbling over our differences, judging our uniqueness and debating our distinctions, let's join together in gratitude and humility for all Jesus has done and what he will do as we unite together in him and for him. He wants to use us all for *his* glory. He wants to change the world through the power of our unity and our selfless faith. Join me as we celebrate the diversity of our oneness and pray for more of *his* power in our unified lives.

*Dear Father, we are grateful that, in your wisdom, you made us in your image with many gifts, abilities and callings. We are forever united in you and purpose to move and breathe as one for the glory of your name. Please help us to see and appreciate the varieties of gifts you have given us. Show us how to honor one another as more important than ourselves, to make room for one another's gifts and to encourage one another daily. We ask you to help us lay down our preferences and destroy our prejudices so that the world may see you in us. We want to represent you and welcome many into your family. We want to strengthen the weak and celebrate those who are moving in the strength you provide.*

*Forgive us for comparison and every type of judgmental measuring. Cleanse us of our need to be right and our desire to win. Help us to lay down our lives for your loved ones and to bear their burdens. We want to see one another through your eyes and hear the longings of our brothers and sisters with your ears. We want to enjoy the diversity you have created and make room for the various expressions of your beauty. Make us one as you and the Father are one, Lord Jesus. Fill us with your Holy Spirit and overwhelm us with love for our God-family as we pursue you together.*

## Prayer Points

Think of brothers and sisters in Christ who have various types of giftings and abilities, and take a moment to thank Jesus for them. Pray for them as God leads.

Ask the Holy Spirit to bring to mind areas where you've failed to appreciate the diversity and variety in the body of Christ. Ask the Lord to show you ways you may encourage those who are unlike you in their gifts and callings.

Pray for areas of prejudice and judgment in your heart toward those in the body of Christ. (Are you judging another church's expression or are you harboring racial prejudice? Are you bitter toward a person or group who has not recognized your calling?) Now is the time to repent and ask Jesus to conform your heart and mind to his perfect will.

Ask God to bring to mind at least one specific person you may encourage in his or her giftings today. Pray for this dear one and write a note, send a text or give them a call to encourage and pray for them.

**In the church, we are to accept and not judge one another when we differ on matters where the Bible does not give specific commandments.**

**— Steven J. Cole**

*Section Four*

# Pray for Families

# Day 19

*Ask God for Supernatural Blessings on Those He Brings Together in Marriage*

---

*Therefore a man shall leave his father and his mother and hold fast to his wife, and they shall become one flesh.*
(**Genesis 2:24**)

---

Genesis 2 gives us the sweetest account of an unexpected twist on God's creative abilities. In the creation story, everything, even the tiniest particle, was made from nothing. It is intriguing to read that Eve, the second human and partner to Adam, was not formed from the dust as he was, but from his very own rib.

From the very beginning, man and woman were miraculously and supernaturally linked. The enemy of our souls has tried every trick in his arsenal to separate and divide husband and wife from one another, but our loving and perfect God destined an inexplicable unity from the very beginning.

It is no accident that Jesus' first miracle was at a wedding. He knows that if the world sees the loving and unbroken union of a husband and wife, it will better understand the devotion that Jesus has for his church. The love Jesus has sacrificially given to his Bride is truly miraculous, and as husbands and wives lay down their lives for one another, a miracle occurs. Two become one powerful force for love and healing in a broken world. Let's pray for supernatural healing and restoration in our marriages so we may not only have the loving life for which we were created, but so that a devastated and lonely world may be drawn to the love of Jesus through our witness.

*Perfect Father, thank you for your wise and loving plan to create man and woman for one another. Thank you for designing marriage as a blessing to families and as a witness of your love for the world. We ask that you bring supernatural love and healing to our marriages.*

*Gracious Father, we need your help to lay down our own selfish desires and your strength to live lives of sacrificial love. We ask you to fill us with your Holy Spirit, so we may encourage and comfort one another. We long for your patience and your truth as we challenge and motivate one another to love and good works. Forgive us for every way we have allowed ourselves to be used to bring discouragement to our mates. Show us how to live in a way that exemplifies the love you and Jesus have for one another. Make us one, supernaturally. Only your power can sustain the love that you have given us. We accept your supernatural anointing on our marriage and vow to live and walk in your power together.*

## Prayer Points

If you are married, ask Jesus to show you a specific reason you and your spouse have been brought together. Thank him for his plan and pray for the next steps in bringing forth his work through your marriage.

If you are single, pray for the marriages in your community and ask Jesus to show you how you may encourage the couples you know.

Pray for the single men and women in your community to be led to and prepared by God for their future mate.

Ask forgiveness for every way you have not honored his plan for your marriage and the marriages of others. Ask Jesus to show you specific ways you may repent.

**God created marriage. No government subcommittee envisioned it. No social organization developed it. Marriage was conceived and born in the mind of God.**

— Max Lucado

## Day 20

Intercede for Father's
and Children's Hearts
to be Turned Toward
One Another

---

*Behold, I will send you Elijah the prophet before the*
*great and awesome day of the* LORD *comes. And he*
*will turn the hearts of fathers to their children and*
*the hearts of children to their fathers, lest I come and*
*strike the land with a decree of utter destruction.*
**(Malachi 4:5–6)**

---

At a Promise Keepers event I heard the most astounding and revealing story. A major greeting card distributor went into a large prison and offered free cards for the inmates to send for Mother's Day. It was a huge success. They ran out of cards.

This greeting card company was so moved that they decided to do the same event for Father's Day. They were shocked to see that even though they brought hundreds of beautiful Father's Day cards to give away free to all the inmates, they had no takers. Zero.

There's nothing more painful or heartbreaking than a father-wound. Let's cry out today for God to heal his people of the deep heart-felt pains resulting from broken relationships with dads.

*Father, I intercede today in keeping with the last prophecy made in the Old Testament (Malachi 4:6) and the first prophecy fulfilled in the New Testament (Luke 1:17)—that you would turn the hearts of the fathers to their children, and the children's hearts to their fathers. Oh, Abba, we are desperate for this move of God to bring healing between fathers and children. We have all experienced the pains of father-wounds, yet we have not all experienced the grace of our heavenly Father bringing healing to our broken hearts and fractured minds. Please bring healing to your people. Even now, you are bringing to mind people in my own family and church who need this work in deep and immediate ways. Heal fathers of the pride, fear, rejection, and anger that paralyzes them from saying, "I am sorry. Please forgive me." Humble and empower children to make the first move to say, "Dad, I love you." Today, I cry out for miracles in family relationships in your people. I ask that lost people would come to Christ and know a blessing on their family that restores broken generations. I trust you, Father, you who are perfect in all your ways, to answer this cry. In Jesus' name, Amen.*

## Prayer Points

Cry out for fathers you know to turn their hearts powerfully and clearly back to their children.

Seek God for children, especially wounded ones, to turn their hearts back to their fathers.

Ask God to provide spiritual fathers and mothers for children, youth, and young adults.

Pray that forgiveness, restoration, and healing would occur in homes across your region.

Believe God for a Jesus awakening in all the homes in your community.

**Fathers, you can have your heart turned away from your children simply by ignoring them. By being so swallowed up in your work that all they get are the dregs of your life.**

— John Piper

# Day 21

⤜⤛

# Pray for Christ-centered Marriages

---

*Wives, submit to your own husbands, as to the Lord. For the husband is the head of the wife even as Christ is the head of the church, his body, and is himself its Savior. Now as the church submits to Christ, so also wives should submit in everything to their husbands. Husbands, love your wives, as Christ loved the church and gave himself up for her, that he might sanctify her, having cleansed her by the washing of water with the word.*
(Ephesians 5:22–26)

---

There's no institution more honored by God than marriage. There's no institution more persecuted by the enemy either. What's the hope for marriages in our communities? Jesus Christ is the answer. "To live is Christ" (Philippians 1:21) is a huge remedy for marriages plagued by dissatisfaction and despair. Are our marriages summarized by Christ? Are our lives filled and overflowing Christ? Is prayer at the heart of our families? Is God's Word celebrated, enjoyed, and rehearsed as a common part of daily life in our homes? The passage above verifies this claim—marriage is about Jesus. He's the heart, soul, mind, and strength of a God-exalting union between man and woman. Jesus is so intimately involved in marriage that he calls our marriages the clearest human picture of his love for the church. The fight for marriages is worth it. What's at stake? Peoples' view of God is at stake. Let's pray for Christ-centered marriages.

*Father, today I lift up marriages in our community. I pray that you would be glorified in the institution of marriage, the beautiful display of the love that your Son Jesus Christ has for his Bride, the church. Bring holy awe back to marriages. I ask today that marriages in my area would be filled with Jesus Christ. That the very life of the marriages would be him—not personality or human will, but you, my Lord. Teach wives to submit to their husbands as the church submits to you. Enable husbands to lead and love as Christ leads and loves the church. May our submission be in Christ. Don't allow husbands to lead their wives into godlessness and don't allow wives to follow their husband into wickedness. I pray for the marriages of Christians today to be a bright and shining light for Jesus. I pray for faithful men and women, sober in our high calling and resolute that our marital unions bring ultimate glory to Jesus Christ. Fill Christian marriages with a sacrificial love, a humble leadership, and a forgiving heart. May husbands nourish and cherish their brides. May wives respond with great joy to follow their husbands in loving, enjoying, and sharing Christ. I ask that the Word of God would fuel godly marriages and would be the foundation for families. Let marriage bring sanctification to each member in the family. I pray each member of the family would fall more and more in love with Jesus. And, in closing, I ask for those wounded by the pain of divorce to find healing in the powerful love of our ever-present Savior, Jesus Christ. In your name I pray, Amen.*

## Prayer Points

Pray for husbands to love their wives as Christ loves the church.

Intercede for wives to respect and follow their husbands as they lead the family.

Seek God for families to be founded on Christ, and that each member would become more Christlike.

Plead with God to glorify his name in Christian marriages.

Cry out to God for healing for those wounded by the pain and trauma of divorce.

**There is no more lovely, friendly or charming relationship, communion or company, than a good marriage.**

— **Martin Luther**

# Day 22

*Pray for Healthy Families*

---

*Children, obey your parents in the Lord, for this is*
*right. "Honor your father and mother" (this is the*
*first commandment with a promise), "that it may go*
*well with you and that you may live long in the land."*
*Fathers, do not provoke your children to anger, but bring*
*them up in the discipline and instruction of the Lord.*
**(Ephesians 6:1–4)**

---

A dear friend of mine at church said, "We all have to overcome our parents' parenting." This was said in humor, but oh, how true it is! All of us have been hurt by our parents. Parenting is the most difficult job in the world. A detailed manual would be nice to have. God has given us clear instructions for children and parents. Today, more than ever, we have moved away from the biblical admonition for parenting. As we intercede today, let's cry out for Jesus to work a new principle or paradigm for parenting into Christian families in your community—a new philosophy of parenting, rooted in God's Word and empowered by the Spirit of God. He is able!

*Father God, a healthy family is a Christ-filled family. Heal our broken families and lead us back to you. Empower dads, moms, and children to take our leads and our guidelines from you and your Word.*

*Today, I ask boldly that you would enable children to obey their parents in the Lord. Cause children in our community to fall so in love with Jesus that they end up leading their parents and siblings to a greater love for Jesus as well. Where families are broken, bring healing to children and teens longing for security in a frightening world. Be their security. Be their home. Be their joy. Send spiritual moms and dads to come alongside parents to love and mentor kids of all ages. Convict parents today of their calling to parent with the love, power, and authority of Jesus Christ. I pray for dads to be stable and involved in the lives of their children. I pray moms will be filled with the Spirit to love their kids practically, with words and deeds. May fathers bring their children up in the discipline and instruction of the Lord. Protect parents from harsh, wounding, or ungodly anger. I plead with you today to give each member of the family a persevering heart, that none would lose their way today. I pray parents would follow the ancient model of talking about Christ all the day, at home or as they travel through the community. May Jesus be a true and relied upon source for families in this community. Protect children from abuse. Protect parents from lives with little to no margins. I am asking today for a powerful move of God in families that are on the brink of divorce, bankruptcy, anger, or depression. Be their solution in real time today. Manifest your glory to families across this region. May we all know that you are God and that your love is better than life itself. Thank you for families. Thank you for my family. Thank you for the families in our great community. We ask for a new and unprecedented work in each one, for Jesus sake. Amen.*

## Prayer Points

Ask God for children in your region to honor and obey their parents.

Pray for parents to love, lead, discipline, and care for their children with all diligence and godliness.

Seek God for healing in broken, divided, and fearful families; pray that God would take the leadership of these families.

Intercede for healthy families to mentor struggling or new families with care and compassion.

Plead with God for perseverance and love of Jesus to be the theme of area families.

Contend in prayer for children to be raised in healthy homes, with the fear and love of the Lord.

> **In addition to teaching your children throughout the day, you must set aside specific, planned times to worship the Lord and learn his Word together. Conducting family devotions requires planning and diligence if this godly practice is to develop and be maintained in your home.**
>
> **— John C. Broger**

# Day 23

## Seek God for Families to Serve the Lord Together

*And if it is evil in your eyes to serve the LORD, choose
this day whom you will serve, whether the gods your
fathers served in the region beyond the River, or the
gods of the Amorites in whose land you dwell. But
as for me and my house, we will serve the LORD.*
**(Joshua 24:15)**

Beautifully illustrated pictures with the verse Joshua 24:15
have hung in the entryways and living rooms of many homes
throughout the years. As a child, I remember reading it daily as I
entered and exited our family's home. I wonder how many of us
have read it but never considered the rewards that would come to
a family who truly lived it. What would be the result of not seeing
it as an invitation to go to Sunday School but as a call to give our
very lives, as a family, to the love and work of Jesus? Would we bear
up under the persecution it would cause, and could we imagine the
generational blessing that this type of dedicated life would provide?

Samuel Wesley knew and lived this verse to the fullest as he and
Susanna raised their nineteen children in the midst of persecution,

illness, and trials of every kind. The unkind treatment this family endured was unthinkable and should have been enough to bring about great doubt and resentment in his children. Instead, John Wesley, the leader of the revival movement that later become the Methodist Church, and Charles Wesley, the writer of over 6,500 hymns, gave their lives to the same gospel their parents had relentlessly proclaimed.

The day in which we live is becoming increasingly evil and the need for our children to be strong in the Lord and the power of his might is becoming more obvious. Let's pray that we, as families, will find the strength that Joshua of the Old Testament and Samuel Wesley of the eighteenth century had. Let's ask Jesus to unite and empower our families to serve him with our whole hearts for our entire lives. One family serving God together could be the tiny spark to light a revival flame. One family praying and believing will bring the change that our lost and dying world needs. Let's pray for the strength and the resolve to serve Jesus as a family.

*Our Father and the Father of generations of believers, thank you for placing us in families. Thank you for making us a powerful unit of love and faith that can change the world. We ask you to light a fire in the hearts of parents and children to know and love you. We ask you to cause us to see serving you as the mission and joy of our lives. More than comfort, entertainment, education or even protection of our lives, cause us to want to know you and make you known.*

*Give us wisdom as we teach our children to love and serve. Help us to make the most of every opportunity to show your truth and your love to this world. Unite us as servants to bring the salvation and healing of the gospel to our neighborhood and our community. Please protect us from the discouragement and temptation that would weaken the bond we share. We ask you to unite us as one for the glory of your name.*

## Prayer Points

Thank Jesus for your family and the families of your community. Be specific in thanking him for the many ways you see him using families to witness and do good for him.

Repent of any way you have led your family in ways that are not in accordance with God's Word and for ways you have failed to model the love of Jesus for your family.

Pray for revival to begin with your family and with the families in your realm of influence.

Pray for God to raise up godly leaders from the next generation.

When parents or couples hang the verse (Joshua 24:15) on the wall in their home today, they are proclaiming very much what Joshua was proclaiming. Parents have a responsibility to make sure what goes on in their home honors God and excludes activities that do not honor or serve him.

— Heather Riggleman

# Day 24

## Contend for Godly Children

---

*Behold, children are a heritage from the L*ORD*,*
*the fruit of the womb a reward.*
*Like arrows in the hand of a warrior*
*are the children of one's youth.*
*Blessed is the man*
*who fills his quiver with them!*
*He shall not be put to shame*
*when he speaks with his enemies in the gate.*
**(Psalm 127:3–5)**

---

Psalm 127:3–5 tells us that our children are like arrows in a warrior's hand, taking down our enemy, waging war against injustice and shining boldly for the glory of his name. These verses, while powerful, prove to be heartbreaking for many as we see the children of most Christians living as less than conquerors. Our God has designed the family to be one of his greatest weapons to wage war against sin and destruction. He has called our children to be mighty in and for him. Let's fight for them in prayer. Let's believe that Jesus can apprehend their hearts and make them revivalists who live with power and love in a weak and hate-filled world.

*Our Father, thank you for our children. We know that it was your providence and your grace that created them and placed them in our families. We are grateful for the honor of raising them, guiding them and loving them. We repent of every way we have failed to honor you in our homes. We ask forgiveness for exalting material gain, social status and even education as more important than knowing you. Today, would you begin a work of deep and lasting change in our children? Would you turn their hearts to you and make them bold witnesses of your love, power and truth? Make them agents of change, weapons of grace in a dark and depraved world. Use them to bring many to salvation. Protect them from every assault of the enemy and embolden them with the power of your word to fight the good fight of faith. Open the eyes of their hearts to know the hope to which you have called them and to live in the inheritance that has been purchased for them through your blood.*

*Give us hearts for adult children who may not have godly parents to pray for them. Open wide our hearts to welcome them into our circles of prayer and to cover them daily. Empower and equip this next generation to wage war against all injustice and to stand strong in the power of your might. Use them to bring revival and to spread the loving message of your gospel throughout the earth. We thank you for sharing this next generation with us; we are grateful to join with them so that all the earth may rejoice in you. In Jesus' name, Amen.*

## Prayer Points

Thank God for the children (young and adult) that he has placed in your family and in your realm of influence. Thank him for the specific gifts and abilities displayed in their lives.

Pray for prodigal children who have wandered from the faith (they may be your own or the adult children of friends). Ask Jesus to encounter them today and to draw them back to him.

Pray for opportunities to be a witness, example and encouragement to children of every age. Ask the Holy Spirit to lead you as you share him with anyone he brings into your life today.

Make a prayer plan to contend in prayer for the children God has placed in your life. Commit to find time every day to pray for their salvation, their protection and their growth in the faith.

> **To train a boy in the way he should go**
> **you must go that way yourself.**
>
> — Billy Sunday

*Section Five*

# Pray for Racial Reconciliation

# Day 25

## Seek Forgiveness for Our Ungodly Distinctions

*For there is no distinction between Jew and Greek;
for the same Lord is Lord of all, bestowing his
riches on all who call on him. For "everyone who
calls on the name of the Lord will be saved."*
**(Romans 10:12–13)**

Every day I face some sort of rejection or separation based upon my skin color." This is the testimony of most of the African-American brothers and sisters that I've visited with over the years. As my dear friend of color, outstanding pastor Fred Moore, told a group of fellow ministers, "Racism is a sin problem, not a skin problem." I am convinced, more than ever, that the praying church (that's you and me today) will be a key factor in knocking down the walls of racial division both in America, and around the world. Let's pray!

*Father God, I cry out to you in the name of Jesus. I'm asking, pleading with you for forgiveness to come to me and to my fellow believers over the sin of making distinctions, especially by race. Jesus, you died to make us one in Christ. Your death and resurrection are mightier, infinitely so, than all our sinful, prejudiced hearts. You have given us new hearts in Jesus Christ. Our new heart has not one, zero, racist part to it. I agree today that I am dead to sin, and dead to all racial distinctions that are rooted in sin and bigotry. In Christ, all those saved by your blood, are of a new race—children of God. No distinction, no separation, and no divisions can succeed over and against your victorious unity purchased on the cross. You removed the dividing wall of hostility between Jews and Gentiles, whites and blacks, Hispanics and Asians, and every other possible division. I celebrate your rich love and overflowing blessings that you have sown into every redeemed believer from any and every tribe and nation. Our distinction is from the world and from the old us, but never between brother or sister in Christ, regardless of their country of origin or color of their skin. I agree with your Word that all who call upon your name can be saved through Jesus Christ. I intercede now for racial groups different from me, and pray that those born in various countries will today hear the gospel and call upon the Lord Jesus for salvation. Forgive, heal, restore, unify, and mobilize your multi-colored church into one new man. I ask this in the name greater than all sin, in the name of Jesus. Amen.*

## Prayer Points

Ask Jesus to forgive you and the believers in your area for our racial divisions.

Seek God for a new work of racial healing, unity, and grace to flow in your region.

Pray for unifiers to arise in the body of Christ who will forge relationships across racial lines.

Intercede for a unity to emerge in the family of God, based solely on our oneness in Christ.

Plead with God for salvation to come to various nations and races in your community.

> Jesus is not calling white to be black or black to be white, but both to be biblical. . . . Biblical truth overrides cultural difference.
>
> — Tony Evans

# Day 26

## Intercede for Racially Diverse Believers to Realize Our Oneness in Christ

---

*There is neither Jew nor Greek, there is neither slave nor free, there is no male and female, for you are all one in Christ Jesus. And if you are Christ's, then you are Abraham's offspring, heirs according to promise.*
(Galatians 3:28–29)

---

I remember the day when I heard Pastor Jim Cymbala correct the pastors in the room, me included, for making distinctions in the body of Christ by highlighting our denominational differences. He said that God doesn't relate to us as Baptists, Pentecostals, Methodists, or any other name. He sees us "in Christ." Denominations are something we've made up, according to Cymbala. It made sense. It also makes sense to apply this same rationale to racial divisions. God doesn't relate to us, nor does he make any distinction between us based upon our skin color or country of origin. He relates to us in Christ. Why do we let race—something that God refuses to divide us over—divide us in the family of God?

*Father, you are the Creator of every tribe and nation, and every skin color known to man. You created us to uniquely display your beauty through a diverse body. Yet we have failed to celebrate our diversity, and have sinfully divided over the color of our skin. We are wicked and need the healing power of Jesus Christ to forgive and restore us. Many have been wounded by racial divisions. And we have been party to some of these wounds. I repent today. I ask that you would so unify your people, of every race and tribe, in Christ Jesus, that the color of our skin and the country of our origin would never be what unites nor divides us. May we reach higher in faith, in keeping with your unchangeable Word, to stop making distinctions and to celebrate our true oneness that you purchased in Christ Jesus.*

*In you, Jesus, there is no black, white, brown, red or yellow. We are simply your people, called by your name. May our relationships simplify around Christ and may divisions fade. In Christ, we are now family. We are eternal family who will live together in the joy of our Master in a new heaven and new earth forever and ever. Nothing will hinder our complete unity. Do this same work now. O Holy Father, I pray for a racial oneness on earth as it is in heaven. I know there are no divisions in heaven. Your people are completely one with you and with one another. Do this sovereign and essential work here, now, in our community. May your church brightly lead the way in humble unity, building relationships across racial and denominational lines. May you glorify your name as your people come together in this challenging hour of human history. May your people lead the way to true and lasting unity through Jesus. Amen.*

## Prayer Points

Intercede for Jesus' people to celebrate that we are all heirs of the promise of God—unified in Christ.

Ask God that his unity will work a true work of healing in our churches, schools, families, and community.

Seek God to give you a close and personal friend of another race or country of origin.

Plead with God for Jesus Christ to be glorified on the earth through his unified people.

> The end that Christ mentions in his prayer for oneness is,
> "that the world may believe" and "that the world may know."
> We cannot hide in the business of evangelism, or feeding
> the hungry, or healing the sick, to avoid what is required of
> us to pursue and realize the oneness of Christ's Church.
>
> — Lauston Stephens

# Day 27

## Living with No Partiality

*And he said to them, "You yourselves know how
unlawful it is for a Jew to associate with or to visit
anyone of another nation, but God has shown
me that I should not call any person common or
unclean." . . . So Peter opened his mouth and
said: "Truly I understand that God shows no
partiality, but in every nation anyone who fears
him and does what is right is acceptable to him."*
(Acts 10:28, 34, 35)

No partiality? Is that even possible for a human in these opinionated and self-focused days? It seems that everywhere we go and everything we read is beckoning us to choose sides and make judgments. The dangerous pride that lurks in the hidden places of each heart tells us that our rights, our thoughts and our culture are king. Jesus has given us a better way. He has opened doors, through his death on the cross, that will free us from the prisons of isolation we have made for ourselves. When he fills our hearts, he also enables us to see his beautiful and varied creation with new lenses of love and acceptance. What a witness we, believers in Jesus, would be to the world if we allowed him to overtake our hearts and minds with his love! Prejudice of every kind is not only sin, it is a poison that will wreck our lives and cause devastation to our communities. The impartial and welcoming love of Jesus is a healing ointment that soothes pain and corrects generational wrongs. Let's repent. Let's turn from our wicked ways. Let's allow Jesus to heal and unite in the way that only he can.

*Loving Father, we love you, and because we love you we want to love the people you love. Forgive us for every way we have shown partiality and harbored prejudice. We know that our sinful pride has separated us and for that, we repent. We ask you to give us your eyes to see those around us. Free us from our dangerously sinful pride. Release us from bitterness toward those who have judged and mistreated us. We want to love as you love. We desire to love without preference and with your generous heart. Help us to take up the cause of those who have no one to defend them. Teach us to fight oppression and seek justice with integrity and humility. Use us to bring reconciliation and healing in our communities. Would you give us fresh ideas as to how we can love? We know the work of restoration is hard and long. Would you empower us to stand for freedom and justice for all and to not grow weary when the battle takes longer than we'd hoped? We know you have called us to live in unity with our brothers and sisters. We believe that you have made us to bring many into your family. Teach us the way of love, Lord Jesus. We honor you and thank you for loving through us. It is in your loving and transformative name we pray and live.*

## Prayer Points

Repent of all the ways you have shown partiality to those with whom you are more comfortable and of every way you have been prejudiced to those who are different from you. (Ask the Lord to bring specific examples and people to mind.)

Think of those who have unfairly mistreated, judged or overlooked you. Forgive them and place them in Jesus' care. Release them from anything you believe they owe you.

Ask the Lord to give you new eyes to see those around you. Listen and watch for specific changes he may bring to your thinking.

Ask the Holy Spirit to show you proactive ways you may be an agent of unity and restoration in your community. As you pray, it may help to write down the ideas God gives you.

**As Christians, for us to reject the despised and the downcast and the overlooked and to receive certain persons because they are considered inherently more worthy of respect is a fundamental contradiction of grace.**

— Ligon Duncan

# Day 28

---

# Refuse to Judge by Appearances

---

*Do not judge by appearances, but*
*judge with right judgment.*
**(John 7:24)**

---

We Christians quickly dispute any notion that we are as judgmental as the world claims, but if we take an honest look at our lives, what do we see? Are we only comfortable with those who share our culture? Are we quick to look down our noses at anyone who holds a different political view than ours? Do whole groups of Christians whose worship looks unlike ours make us squirm? It seems that we have taken our preferences and our assumptions based on outward appearance to a level that would mirror idolatry. We desire our comfort and our opinions more than we want to see Jesus worshiped and his love shared with the entire world. The book of John tells us that Jesus died because God so loved the world. What prejudices and preferences can we put aside to share the gospel? If Jesus truly died for everyone and his love is available to anyone, how can we possibly see that one we judge through any eyes but his? We must ask Jesus to give us his eyes to see and his heart to love all for whom he died.

*Precious Jesus, we love you. Because we love you, we want you to teach us to love all whom you love. Thank you for dying on the cross for us, and also for those we judge. We repent of selfishness, fear, and prejudice of every kind. Please forgive us for the pride that convinces us that we know the deepest part and ultimate destiny of every individual. Only you know the plans you have for those you have created. Only you know how to bring us all to the purpose for which we were made. Enlighten the eyes of our hearts that we may live with a hope not only for ourselves but for those around us. Help us to trust your power to bring about the work you have for all of your people. Show us how to help those who are weak, encourage the strong and love everyone. There is no way we can do any of this on our own. Fill us with your Spirit today so we may believe you for your work of unity in our community. Strengthen us so we may fight for the oppressed and forgive the oppressor. Give us patience and endurance to believe when the change we all need is slow in coming. Give us love to cover the sins that so easily entangle us all; give us hope to believe that you are working a mighty plan of restoration in our lives. We love you, Jesus. Show us how to love our brothers and sisters, in your name.*

## Prayer Points

Ask the Holy Spirit to bring to mind individuals and groups you have wrongly judged. Ask him to give you his perspective of them so you may view them through Jesus' eyes. (Don't rush this. Take time to let the Lord show you your wrong judgments.)

Repent of every way you have allowed your judgment to separate you from those Jesus loves. Be specific and open to everything God shows you.

Ask the Lord to show you how to judge people and situations rightly.

Pray for a group or person whom you find difficult to pray for. Ask Jesus for his heart and perspective.

**I judge all things only by the price they shall gain in eternity.**

— John Wesley

# Day 29

## Dealing with Hatred

*Whoever says he is in the light and hates his brother is
still in darkness. Whoever loves his brother abides in
the light, and in him there is no cause for stumbling.*
**(1 John 2:9–10)**

Merriam Webster's definition of hate cuts to the chase. Hatred
is said to be intense hostility or aversion usually deriving from
fear, anger, or sense of injury. The word aversion indicates that our
heart chooses to turn away from someone because we are repulsed
and find them distasteful.

Nowhere is hatred more obvious and more insidious than when
it is directed toward one of God's beautiful people simply based on
the race he chose for them. The ugliness of racism affects us all and
can be seen in every community in our land. Sometimes resulting
from injury and always fed by ignorance, the hatred that stems from
prejudice will kill us and devastate our communities.

How offended must our loving God feel when we take the grace
to live, breathe and love that we've been given and use our freedoms
to mistreat those for whom he died! How it must break his heart to
see his beloved children making excuses for and stoking the fire of
hate in our hearts!

It's easy to judge the things we don't understand about another culture, but it is also dangerous and deadly. It is easy to rationalize our prejudices and call them something other than hate, but the Bible is clear that if we don't love our brother we are not loving God. Let's ask Jesus to give us his love for those he loves, and to overwhelm our hearts with his affection and understanding for his children.

*Loving Father, we need your love to cleanse us of every sinful thought that separates us from those you love. Show us the hidden disdain in our hearts. We ask you to forgive us for every way we have distanced ourselves from one another and to cleanse us of even the smallest prejudice. We know that you created us all in your image and that your image is perfect and complete. Show us the beauty in each person we encounter and give us a glimpse of the glory you have hidden in them.*

*Forgive us for considering our ways, our culture and ourselves as more important than our fellow man. Show us how to lay down our lives for one another and to stand our ground in defending those who have been oppressed and overlooked. Let the love you have for us flow through us to every hurting heart. Make us one as you and Jesus are one. Teach us how to bridge gaps that have been created by the hatefulness and misunderstanding that we as a society have built. Make us ministers of reconciliation for the glory of your name and give us wisdom as to how we can unite for your purposes. Please show us, today, specific ways we may bring healing and reconciliation to our community and give us the strength to walk out your plans. We thank you for bringing us brothers and sisters from every tribe and nation and we resolve, today, to love your children in your name and through your power.*

## Prayer Points

Ask the Lord to bring to mind groups of people you have hated or failed to love. Repent specifically for every way you have harbored prejudice in your heart.

Repent of ways you have failed to act or reach out on behalf of those from other cultures or races. Repent of any unforgiveness you have held toward any person or group.

Ask the Holy Spirit to give you his insight to allow you to see these people through his eyes. Pray for specific insight into their lives, gifts and needs.

Pray for a plan to help bring reconciliation in your community and ask Jesus to show you what he would have you do. Prayerfully, write your thoughts here.

> **Darkness cannot drive out darkness: only light can do that. Hate cannot drive out hate: only love can do that.**
>
> **— Martin Luther King, Jr.**

# *Day 30*

✦

# Celebrating Every
# Tribe and Nation

---

*After this I looked, and behold, a great multitude
that no one could number, from every nation, from
all tribes and peoples and languages, standing
before the throne and before the Lamb, clothed in
white robes, with palm branches in their hands.*
(Revelation 7:9)

---

God must love diversity. He created us so beautifully different,
all to reflect his multifaceted glory. His splendor cannot be
contained, but we can reflect it in our God-glorifying qualities that
he both created and recreated in us to display his unmatched immi-
nence. All of history groans, waiting for the day when all will be
made "right," and the new order will forever be in place under the
headship of Christ. On that day, around the throne of God, we will
see people from every tribe, nation, and people group that have ever
existed, each one saved by the blood of Jesus through the preaching
of the gospel by believers worldwide. All the pains of the past will
crescendo into a glorious, unified, radiant, diverse body of Christ

where everyone will be overflowing in ceaseless praise! Let's pray toward that day.

*Father, today we hurt over our racial, ethnic, and political divisions. We long for the day when all your blood-bought body of Christ will stand in complete unity around your effervescent throne, with thunder and lighting filling the heavenly atmosphere. We celebrate that you have intricately and purposely created us all in your image. We refuse to speak against anyone made in your image—which includes all people. We celebrate all races. I praise you for those that are black. I rejoice in those who are brown. I cheer for those who are white. I applaud those who are yellow. Obliterate any hint of racism in my family, your church, and my community. You call us to live "on earth as it is in heaven." In heaven all ethnic groups, all nations, all people groups are crying out in unison—Holy is the Lord God Almighty! The divisions will be over. May that occur right here and right now; may the backbiting be gone; may it end now. All superiority and oppression will cease. May it be no more in our time, in our city, in our family. To love as we have been loved is the goal and joy of heaven—I plead for this to be done now through your people. Forgive my passive love. Forgive my divided allegiances. Forgive my shortsighted judgments. I ask today that you empower your church to celebrate our unique color, backgrounds, voices, languages, nationalities, and appearance; and allow us, together, to look to you as our unifying joy forevermore. Amen.*

## Prayer Points

Praise God for the beautiful, multicolored, and multiethnic body of Christ in your area.

Forgive those who have been prejudiced against you. Ask for forgiveness for your prejudice.

Seek God for his leadership in leading you to one person of another race you can bless this week.

Pray big prayers: Ask that God's will be done concerning unity and love between races "on earth as it is in heaven."

Rejoice in God that he will make his diverse body one!

> By the grace of the Holy Spirit, we need to
> cultivate compassion for those outside our tribe.
> We must learn not simply to tolerate them,
> but to value and celebrate and love them.
>
> — Subby Szterszky

*Section Six*

# Pray for Life to Be Valued and Protected through All Stages of Life, Beginning at Conception

# Day 31

Knit Together in My
Mother's Womb

---

*For you formed my inward parts;*
*You knitted me together in my mother's womb.*
*I praise you, for I am fearfully and wonderfully made;*
*Wonderful are your works;*
*my soul knows it very well.*
*My frame was not hidden from you,*
*when I was being made in secret,*
*intricately woven in the depths of the earth;*
*Your eyes saw my unformed substance;*
*in your book were written, every one of them,*
*the days that were formed for me,*
*when as yet there was none of them.*
**(Psalm 139:13–16)**

---

The thought of a tiny, but growing, human being hiding in the secret place while being watched only by the God of the universe is beautiful and awe-inspiring. The reality that the same God is intricately weaving a body and a life-plan too detailed and perfect for words is beyond comprehension. The understanding that, at any moment, that precious developing child could be stolen from a world who needs his life and his ordained contribution is heart-breaking. Let's pray to the Creator of every beautiful life and ask for an understanding of his plan for every baby he will create. Let's ask to view all of life, from the womb to the tomb, with his vision of promise and dignity. Let's commit our hearts and prayers to fighting for those he so carefully creates and constantly loves.

*Wise and loving Father, we ask you to open our eyes and enlarge our hearts to see and understand the beauty of life at every stage. We thank you that, in your perfect wisdom, you have chosen to form us detail by detail in the secret place of your love and your protection. We ask you to forgive us for every way we have failed to protect all of the ones you love. Give us hearts to understand the power of your purpose for their lives and the resolve to ensure their protection at every stage of life. We pray for compassionate and proactive hearts to help women facing an unplanned pregnancy as we know that every day of their lives is also wanted and planned by you. Take away all judgment from our hearts and give us a desire to walk with those who are faced with an unknown future. Help us to stand for the unborn. Show us how we may help and love both mother and baby to become the powerful light bearers you intend.*

## Prayer Points

Ask God to forgive you for every way you have neglected the pre-born and their mothers.

Pray for an end to abortion and a heart to help bring this about.

Pray for women in your community who may be faced with the unthinkable decision today. Ask Jesus to send people of grace to guide, support and care for them and their babies.

Pray for babies who are scheduled to be aborted today. Pray for their protection and that Jesus will provide all that they need to grow into his image.

> I do not believe the promises of the Declaration of Independence are just for the strong, the independent, the healthy. They are for everyone—including unborn children.
>
> — George W. Bush

# Day 32

❦

# Set Apart Before Birth

---

*Now the word of the LORD came to me, saying,*
*"Before I formed you in the womb I knew you,*
*and before you were born I consecrated you; I*
*appointed you a prophet to the nations."*
(Jeremiah 1:4–5)

---

God, our infinite Creator, does not react or get surprised. All that he does is done with absolute and perfect purpose. The knitting together of a baby in a mother's womb follows this same purposeful and wise pattern. No child is a mistake, regardless of the time or circumstances surrounding his or her conception. Humans can have sexual relations, but only God makes babies. Our God is intimately involved in all he creates and sustains all things by his mighty power. Today we continue our prayers for the unborn. Nothing could be more vitally important in this season. Pray. Forgive. Be forgiven. Our God is the giver of life—life forevermore.

*Father, just as you knew Jeremiah before he was formed, you consecrated and appointed him as a prophet to the nations. Forgive me and forgive my nation for the lack of prophetic insight by which we characterize the unborn. Forgive us for the passive ways we defend the most defenseless in our society. Forgive me for not speaking up for those who cannot speak for themselves*

*(Proverbs 31:8–9). Before I was born you knew me. Before I took a breath, you consecrated and appointed me for good works that you planned before the world was even created (Ephesians 2:10). I intercede today for unborn children whose lives are in the balance. I pray that moms would be dissuaded from abortion today across our community, state, and nation. Empower those who are even now fighting to save unborn children from the throes of death. Rescue, O Father, children yet to be born for which you have destined purposes unknown. We trust you. You do not create anything that is without purpose. Forgive us for our human wisdom that considers some lives, old or young, useless and expendable. Breathe life into our land. Convict humans that each and every life has infinite value and worth. Heal our land of the atrocity of abortion and the tragedy of euthanasia. Restore life as valuable in each and every phase of life. As we honor life, we honor you. We cry out for great mercy on our broken land today. Heal our land. In Jesus' name, Amen.*

## Prayer Points

Ask Father God to raise up a modern William Wilberforce who will fight unrelentingly for the unborn. Ask to be one in your community.

Seek forgiveness for being passively pro-life. Ask God for next steps in being actively pro-life.

Pray for leaders, pastors, and Christians in your region to join together in unity for the sake of the unborn and children in need.

Intercede for godly and healthy Christian families to answer the call to foster and adopt children.

Cry out for neglected elderly people in your area to be loved, valued, cared for, and treasured.

**I've noticed that everyone who is for
abortion has already been born.**
**— Ronald Reagan**

# *Day 33*

꧁꧂

# Rescue Those Being
# Taken to Death

---

*Rescue those who are being taken away to death;*
*hold back those who are stumbling to the slaughter.*
**(Proverbs 24:11)**

---

What an astounding command! Rescue those who are being taken away to death. Most Christians know very little about how to rescue the unborn or those who are left to die alone in their old age. We are most often preoccupied with our lives, our families, our jobs, our neighbors, our churches, and so on. Today, may we think through and pray through how we can directly apply Proverbs 24:11 to rescue the unborn or those left to die unjustly. In 2008, my wife and I saw a group standing in front of our neighborhood abortion clinic praying for the end of abortion. "Does that really work?" was my honest thought. After more than a decade of standing and praying in front of abortion clinics in greater Austin with a handful of believers many times yearly, we have seen hundreds of babies rescued. I'm not advocating this as the only way, just one way. Let's pray and ask to rescue those being taken to death in our community, in our state, in our nation.

*Jesus, you said, "Let the little children come to me, for such is the kingdom of heaven." I ask today, Lord Jesus, that you would help us obey Proverbs 24:11 and rescue those being led to slaughter. I ask for the power, the means, the plan, the partnership, and the love to see evil and death defeated at the abortion clinic, and in the minds of women who are facing unexpected pregnancies and feel they have no choice. Jesus, you can make a way where there is no way. That's what I am interceding for today. Rescue those being led to death today in our city, state, and nation. Intercede through your people, your Word, or any way you choose to empower scared and shaken moms and dads to choose life. This topic is so very difficult for the many who have bought the lie that their only real choice is to end a life. Lord Jesus, you once lived in your mother's womb and an evil king sought to kill you before and after you were born. Father, you rescued your Son. Rescue sons and daughters today in our community. I ask this with my whole heart. Amen.*

## Prayer Points

Pray that Christians will agree with God's Word about the value of life in all stages and forms.

Seek God now for women and men leaning toward abortion to change their minds and choose life for their babies.

Intercede for churches in your area to once again preach about the sin of abortion and the mercy of God for those who have had or were complicit in one.

Cry out now for love to drive us in all our pro-life activities.

Plead with God to give you and other Christians divine appointments with those facing life-and-death decisions in your community, family, and world.

**Christ died that we might live. This is the opposite of abortion. Abortion kills that someone might live differently.**

**— John Piper**

## Day 34

## Cleanse the Community of Shedding Innocent Blood

---

*"'Accept atonement, O LORD, for your people Israel, whom you have redeemed, and do not set the guilt of innocent blood in the midst of your people Israel, so that their blood guilt be atoned for.' So you shall purge the guilt of innocent blood from your midst, when you do what is right in the sight of the LORD."*

(**Deuteronomy 21:8–9**)

---

The cry of over sixty million aborted babies stands against us as a nation. Worldwide, several billion have been sacrificed at the altar of convenience. Who will atone for this needless bloodshed? Jesus has made a way for all sin to be covered. Only Jesus' blood can reverse the curse of the shedding of innocent blood. As intercessors, our cry is for mercy over our community, city, and nation. We become watchmen on the walls, pleading as Moses did in the days of old, for God not to destroy our land because of our wickedness. In ancient Jerusalem, Gehenna was the valley known as "hell," where parents went to kill their children. It's still thought to be a cursed valley in modern Jerusalem. Today, let's cry out for repentance, for restoration, for salvation, and for a healed land. Let's ask God for babies to be given the right to live and to know our Jesus on this earth.

*Father, we plead your blood over our nation. We ask you to forgive us for the needless murder of over sixty million children who were created in your image. Please bring an end to the wholesale slaughter of the unborn. Forgive me and forgive us for the ways we've minimized the horrific practice of abortion. We have one hope—that is you, Lord Jesus. If we cover our sin, what hope remains? If we deny our part, even in voting or in passivity, how can redemption occur? Awaken your people, your churches, and my community to the vital truth that all life must be valued from conception to natural death. Where policies and traditions exist that violate this truth, we ask that you, O King, would intervene and heal our land. Jesus, your blood is more powerful than the blood we've shed as a nation. Your grace is greater than our sin. Your power to forgive and heal trumps our weak and broken ways. You are the hope of America, the world, and my little community. Today, let me be a Spirit-empowered advocate for life. Use me to save babies, care for the fatherless, serve the widows, and provide for the aging. Let a culture of life overcome the culture of death that pervades our land. We need a great awakening! You can do it, Lord. Begin with me. Start now. In Jesus' name, Amen.*

## Prayer Points

Ask for forgiveness on behalf of our nation for the millions aborted in our land.

Seek God for a culture of life to be established in our families, schools, churches, and governing bodies.

Intercede for God to expose the atrocity of abortion in America and to bring unshakable conviction across the entire nation, causing a nationwide repentance.

Believe God that his blood shed for us all would result in mercy over our land. Pray for God's mercy to turn America and your specific community back to him.

Cry out for God to bring a third great awakening to our world, beginning with you, your family, and community.

> How many others suffered in silence, too ashamed and too afraid to speak about their pain? The world wouldn't let them grieve for children they had aborted. How could they when the rhetoric said there was no child? How does one grieve what doesn't exist? No one wanted to admit the truth.
>
> — Francine Rivers

# Day 35

## Let the Little Children Come To Jesus

*But when Jesus saw it, he was indignant and said to them, "Let the children come to me; do not hinder them, for to such belongs the kingdom of God."*
(Mark 10:14)

The disciples wanted to stop the disruptions of children who were being brought to Jesus. They surely reasoned that he needed to be about God's more important work of healing, casting out demons, and performing miracles. Jesus knew the truth that childlike faith and total dependence on him are the keys to the kingdom. He lovingly touched and blessed the children because he loves their tender hearts and their open minds to receive fully from him. Jesus loves the little children. We've sung the song, but have we lived its truth? Have we prioritized children the way Jesus does? Have we made a way in our hearts, our actions and even our homes for them to learn of and receive from him? Today, our hearts are faced with the reality that our society sees children in much the same way as the disciples. We want children to join us when they are convenient and fit into our preconceived plans. Jesus wants us to live like little children, full of faith and dependence trusting that his ways are best. Let's pray for the safety and the comfort of children at every stage of life, from the womb to adulthood. Let's commit our hearts and lives to fight in prayer for their access to the One who loves them and always welcomes them.

*Dear Jesus, thank you for the way you love the little children. Thank you for your protection and heart of access toward them. Thank you for always seeing them and making a way for them to touch you. We ask you to give us your heart for children at every stage of life. We need you to change our hearts and minds from our selfish predispositions to those of love and welcome for children at every stage of life. We repent for not fighting for their right to live and we ask forgiveness for not making their well-being a priority. Help us to not just claim to be pro-life but enable us to lay down our comforts so that children at every stage may have everything they need to grow into the lives you've designed for them. Show us how to welcome them into this beautiful God-family and give us the resources we need to share our lives with them. We love you, Jesus, and we want to love your children well. Please flow through us and touch the children today with your love, your healing, and your empowerment. We ask this in your protective and nurturing name.*

## Prayer Points

Thank Jesus for the little children in your community (Be specific as you think of children he has shared with you).

Pray for a heart to see and love children as Jesus does. Ask him to open your eyes to the needs of children around you.

Pray for forgiveness for neglecting to make way for children to have access to Jesus.

Ask the Father to show you where you can serve on behalf of children. Does he want you to pray for an end to abortion, pray for specific children and families, teach a Sunday School class, mentor at a school, or even provide a meal for a young family in your community?

> It is a masterpiece of the devil to make us believe that children cannot understand religion. Would Christ have made a child the standard of faith if he had known that it was not capable of understanding his words?
>
> — Dwight L. Moody

*Section Seven*

# Pray for Local
# and National
# Governmental Leaders

# Day 36

## Interceding for those who Govern

*First of all, then, I urge that supplications, prayers, intercessions, and thanksgivings be made for all people, for kings and all who are in high positions, that we may lead a peaceful and quiet life, godly and dignified in every way.*
(1 Timothy 2:1–2)

The highest place and the most influential vocation is that of intercessor. From our humble homes and lowly hearts, we are able to influence kings and nations, to change history. Why would God give such power to our prayers? The answer is vast, but one reason is he gives us a small part in joining him in ruling the universe through prayer. As we cry out today, we will be seeking God on behalf of our President, Congress, Senate, governors, mayors, and all those who rule on a local level. Through prayer, we have been invited to shape history and influence world events. Let us enter this high calling of prayer with a humble and contrite heart, never praying from a place of pride or selfish anger, but seeking the highest good for those who govern our nation and community, as well as for those who are being governed. Let's pray.

*Father, we follow your Word, which commands us to pray for kings and for those in high positions. As you said, we start with* **supplications**— *seeking that every need of those who govern would be met by Christ and that he would become their Lord and Savior. Our* **prayers** *for them are that every leader would know the love of Jesus today—that their decisions would be rooted in this heavenly love, and that wisdom from heaven would pervade their thoughts, meetings, and each decision. Our* **intercessions** *are for your kingdom to come and your will to be done on earth as it is in heaven through these leaders' governing. Establish your government through their leadership. I join with other intercessors today offering* **thanksgivings** *for the leaders you have put in office. Bless them beyond what they deserve. May your grace and justice be the clear guide as they govern nationally and locally. Glorify your name through each and every leader from the President of the United States to the president of the local parent-teacher organization. Enable me to be a faithful and fruitful watchman on the wall for our governing leaders. Shine brightly as they lead. May righteousness exalt our nation today. In the name of Jesus. Amen.*

## Prayer Points

Seek forgiveness for every rude or negative word you've spoken about your leaders.

Ask for God to use our governing officials to bring ultimate glory to his name.

Pray that these leaders would humble themselves, pray, seek God's face, and would turn from their wicked ways.

Cry out for God to use these leaders to be a part of healing our land in this hour.

Intercede for God's specific and powerful blessings to rest on each leader as they get to know Jesus as Savior and Lord.

**It is impossible to rightly govern a nation
without God and the Bible.**

**— George Washington**

# Day 37

## Be Subject to the Governing Authorities

*Let every person be subject to the governing authorities.*
*For there is no authority except from God, and*
*those that exist have been instituted by God.*
**(Romans 13:1)**

In our current political climate, verses like Romans 13:1 sound like a Pollyanna dream from long ago. Can God actually call his people to "be subject to the governing authorities"? We see so many specific errors being propagated by our leaders that it makes it difficult for us to embrace this simple, clear command from God to his people. Yet, the next sentence sheds more light on why God calls us to submit to our leaders—he himself instituted them. God is the Authority behind our authorities. Granted, God never makes agreement or is ever to blame for legislated evil or wickedness of any kind. Our calling is to "be subject," to submit or place ourselves under in rank of those who govern over us. They are accountable to God and we are to them as long as they obey his Word. We are always called to stand against evil in government, in society, and in our very own lives. Yet, God's call to submit is to work a work of humility in his people. Let's pray about this truth.

*Heavenly Father, may we as your people learn submission to you by submitting to the governing authorities. I ask today that we, your children, would live such godly, submissive lives that we would be a great blessing to the church, the world, and to those who rule over us. Forgive me for my times of rebellion against the righteous laws of the land and for speaking evil against those you instituted to govern over us. Righteous King, I cry out for your people to be salt and light today, even to those who lead us. May your people help to transform our country through living and preaching of the gospel of Jesus Christ. Teach us humility, submission, and to be subject to those who rule over us as unto you. We submit to our leaders out of reverence for Christ. Shine brightly in our nation through your humble, righteous, kind, and contagious church. May the best part of our nation be the fruit born out of the prayers and labors of those called by your name. Exalt your name through our nation. Save leaders. Empower godly leaders. Rebuke false leaders. Overturn unjust laws. Transform the heart, soul, and mind of our nation through the power of the risen Christ. I pray these things in Jesus' name. Amen.*

## Prayer Points

Thank God that he is revealing his authority by instituting governing leaders.

Intercede for God to make godly leaders out of those who govern and to call godly men and women to run for office.

Ask for enabling power to be subject to those who lead in all areas of life, unless the leaders are asking for ungodly actions.

Cry out for the body of Christ in America to be deeply humbled under God's mighty hand.

Pray for God's people, his church, to be the most transforming influence in our nation.


**Freedom prospers when religion is vibrant and the rule of law under God is acknowledged.**

— Ronald Reagan

# *Day 38*

❧

# Honor Those Who Govern

---

*Honor everyone. Love the brotherhood.*
*Fear God. Honor the emperor.*
**(1 Peter 2:17)**

---

These four commands of Scripture will revolutionize our lives if both understood and obeyed. *Honor everyone.* Honor means to esteem, value at a price, or reverence. Biblically it is considering others as more important than ourselves. *Love your brothers and sisters.* This is seeking the highest good of others through Christ. *Fear God.* Stand in holy awe of our God. *Honor the emperor.* This is the greatest challenge of them all and seems counterintuitive to our normal way of thinking. Reverence your leaders, your president, mayor, or governor as someone appointed by God and pray for their success in governing wisely.

*Father, today we have lost our sense of honor. At this moment I begin to honor you, reverence you, and esteem you above all. I esteem and submit to your perfect Word, even when I do not fully understand it. Enable me and your people to honor everyone. Forgive me now for the specific ways I have dishonored others in word and deed. Empower me to love my brothers and sisters in Christ. Give me specific ways to both treasure them and practical ways to serve them in this season. I cry out today for holy fear of God to be brought back to your church. Teach us to trust you with all our hearts and to lean not on our own understanding. May the awe of you and your name take root in your people so we once again will be known as those who fear you. You know that we live in a season when dishonor is far more common than honor. To honor those who lead us as president, mayor, and governor seems insincere and tainted with evil. Forgive me and forgive us for vilifying those you've placed in office and those who are running for office. Give us the gift of honor, so we can learn to esteem even those with whom we disagree by displaying your love and grace towards them in word and deed. Right that which is wrong in me, in my family, community, and city. Display honor and grace through my life and choices today. In Jesus' name, Amen.*

## Prayer Points

Seek forgiveness for any and all dishonor of others.

Ask God to give you tangible love to display toward his people. Ask for a specific assignment today.

Plead with God that fear of his name will be restored to you, your family, church, and community.

Request power and grace to display honor for the President, governor, and mayor today.

Intercede for your church and community to experience and live a life of honor to others.

> **Obedience to the will of God is the pathway
> to perpetual honor and everlasting joy.**
> — Charles Spurgeon

# Day 39

## Be Submissive to the Governing Authorities

*Remind them to be submissive to rulers and authorities,*
*to be obedient, to be ready for every good work, to*
*speak evil of no one, to avoid quarreling, to be gentle,*
*and to show perfect courtesy toward all people.*
(Titus 3:1–2)

The verses above are as foreign to most of us as the Greek language in which they were originally written. In this day of political fighting, disregard for authority, and rebellion against every type of leader, the need to follow and honor leaders seems to be mostly ignored. How can we show and shine the light of Jesus in a dark and depraved world if we carry the same dim attitudes and speak the same hate-clouded talk as those who have not yet embraced our Savior? Are we ready for good work? Are we speaking evil of those with whom we disagree? Are we picking fights with those who hold different opinions than the ones to which we so tightly cling? Does the world know we are Christians by the love we have for one another and by the grace we show to every man, woman and child? Let's ask the Holy Spirit to invade our minds, cleanse our hearts and give us speech that honors God.

*Holy Spirit, we repent of every way that we have played God as we've chosen to pick and choose whom we honor. We ask you to forgive us for putting our agendas and our preferences above your call to witness of your goodness and your grace. Give us faith in the place of the fear that often drives our lack of submission and our unkind speech. Help us to love as you love and to regard everyone with your discernment and hope. Let us shine as lights in this dark world and lead many to you through our grace-filled lives. When our authorities rule in opposition to your Word, give us the wisdom to know how to honor your truth with courtesy and without compromise. We pray for and trust in your protection from evil as we uphold your Word. We know that you have the best plan for our lives and are able to keep us in the center of your will. We trust you, Jesus. We honor you, Father. We listen to you, Holy Spirit.*

## Prayer Points

Repent for every way you have dishonored your leaders in speech and actions. (Ask the Lord to show you specific instances in which you've had dishonoring attitudes and speech.)

Repent for the lack of faith that causes you to try to win spiritual battles with earthly weapons instead of putting on the whole armor of God and trusting him to care for you.

Ask the Holy Spirit to show you specific leaders for whom you may pray and commit to praying regularly for them.

Pray for opportunities to honor and witness to leaders at your job, at your church, in your community and anywhere else God leads.

Democracy is not prescribed in the Bible, and
Christians can and do live under other political systems.
But Christians can hardly fail to love democracy,
because of all systems it best assures human dignity,
the essence of our creation in God's image.

— Charles W. Colson

## Day 40

Seek Justice Through Government

*He has told you, O man, what is good;*
*and what does the Lord require of you*
*but to do justice, and to love kindness,*
*and to walk humbly with your God?*
(Micah 6:8)

We live in a time filled with confusion, mistrust and of seemingly never-ending power plays. Our society is needy for rulers who will rule with integrity, wisdom and compassion. Our communities are being torn apart by prejudice of every kind and unimaginably evil acts and decisions. We need leaders who will put the needs of people and the heart of God at the forefront of their decisions. We are longing for elected and appointed officials who walk with integrity in the secret places and shine a bright light of truth from public platforms. God has given us a clear mandate for our prayers. In Micah 6:8, he has shown us three of the areas we must contend to see in the lives, hearts and decisions of our leaders. As we vote, we must pray. As we serve, we must pray. As we submit, we must pray. Our God is ready and willing to move in our hearts and in the hearts of our leaders.

*Almighty God, ruler of all, we thank you that you govern and lead with perfect love and wisdom. We thank you that you are ruling in ways that we cannot imagine and in places unknown to bring about your will in all the earth. We submit to you as the One true ruler and ask you to bring about your will on earth as it is in heaven. We humble ourselves before you and ask you to forgive us for every way we have judged our rulers wrongly. We know that we only see a small glimpse of what you are doing and need you to direct us as we pray. Help us to honor you as we honor and pray for our leaders. We ask you to lead them into all* **justice***, and to move their hearts and minds to conform to the truths of your Word. Give them integrity in the secret parts of their lives and give them the strength to live out that integrity as they make decisions that affect our communities. Give them hearts of compassion and* **kindness** *so they may help those who are most needy and may also empower those who have ability to use their resources to help. Give our leaders* **humility** *so they may seek you and the good that you provide for those you love. Protect them from the temptation to make a name for themselves and deliver them from the evil of ungodly and self-seeking compromise. Raise up new leaders who will govern with justice, kindness and humility. Tear down idolatry in every place it has taken hold and allow true worship of you to arise. Bring revival to our leaders in every seat of justice and let it flow to the people they lead. We expect you to move in every political party and for all people. We are watching. We are waiting. We are ready to serve you in our communities. We are your people and we pray these things in your all-powerful name.*

## Prayer Points

Pray for leaders that the Holy Spirit brings to your mind. Pray Micah 6:8 for them.

Repent of every way you have wrongly judged and criticized the leaders of our land.

Ask Jesus to raise up new leaders who carry his heart for your community.

Ask the Lord to show you areas where you may serve your leaders and community and pray for wisdom and strength to obey.

**Injustice anywhere is a threat to justice everywhere.**

— **Martin Luther King, Jr.**

# AFTERWORD

## By Brian Alarid
### President of America Prays & World Prays

Now that you have begun praying the Word over your city, we want to invite you to adopt a monthly day of prayer and join a movement of unceasing prayer that began in Austin, Texas twelve years ago and is sweeping across our nation.

America Prays is a movement of believers and churches covering America in 24/7 prayer. Our vision is to unite and equip 40,000 churches in 24/7 prayer for a national spiritual awakening. We are a multiethnic, interdenominational, multigenerational, Jesus-centered prayer movement.

J. Edwin Orr once said, "No great spiritual awakening has begun anywhere in the world apart from united prayer." The world is in desperate need of spiritual awakening. Will you stand in the gap for your community and our nation?

We encourage churches to have a weekly prayer meeting, adopt a monthly day of prayer, connect with other pastors and churches once a quarter for prayer, fellowship, and inspiration, and gather for united prayer annually on the National Day of Prayer.

You can join this prayer movement by adopting a monthly day of prayer for your church or ministry.

## Simple Steps to Launch A Day of Prayer

1. **ADOPT A DAY OF PRAYER:** Sign up at AmericaPrays.org for a monthly full day of prayer (24 hours) or half-day of prayer (12 hours). Your church or ministry will pray the same day of the month (1st, 8th, etc.) or day of the week (Second Wednesday, Fourth Friday, etc.).

2. **APPOINT A PRAYER COORDINATOR:** The prayer coordinator is a member of the church, who under the leadership of the pastor, organizes, schedules, and provides general leadership for the church's prayer activities (including the day of prayer). This person needs an active and healthy prayer life, a good reputation in and outside of the church, and the ability to lead in prayer and mobilize others to pray.

3. **SHARE THE VISION:** The pastor shares the vision with the church during Sunday morning services a few weeks before the first day of prayer. Points to include:

• Share the goals behind the day of prayer
• Affirm the prayer coordinator and his/her role
• Encourage people to sign up to pray for 30 or 60 minutes

4. **RECRUIT AND FOLLOW UP:** Using prayer commitment cards, signup sheets, or mobile signup during or after services, have people sign up for a prayer time slot. Print and distribute simple prayer points to those who sign up (suggestions on how to pray during their committed prayer time, including specific and measurable prayer points to pray for the church, city, and state).

The prayer coordinator follows up with those who sign up (through text, email, or the church's preferred method of communication), with prayer points, scheduled time reminders, encouragement, etc. and works on getting all the time slots filled by prayer partners.

**5. PRAY:** Prayer partners pray from home, school, work, church, or anywhere. This will help them make prayer a daily lifestyle.

# SIMPLE STEPS TO LAUNCH
# A DAY OF PRAYER

| 1 | 2 | 3 | 4 | 5 |
|---|---|---|---|---|
| Pastor selects a half or full day for the church to pray every month. | Pastor appoints a Prayer Coordinator to manage the day of prayer and volunteers. | Pastor shares the vision with the church on a Sunday morning a few weeks before the first day of prayer. | Church members sign up to pray for 30 or 60 minutes on the chosen day of prayer. | Coordinator sends reminders and volunteers pray from home, work, school or church. |

# ABOUT THE AUTHORS

## Trey Kent

Trey and Mary Anne Kent planted Northwest Fellowship in 1993, where Trey is the senior pastor. He has been in full-time ministry since 1986. Trey has a Master of Divinity from Oral Roberts University and did doctorate work at Fuller Seminary. His passions are Jesus, prayer and his family. He is the proud husband of Mary Anne and the grateful father of daughters Lindsay, Christina and son-in-law, Nick, and doting grandfather to two amazing grandsons, Samuel and Levi. In 2009, God led Trey to launch the Unceasing Prayer Movement mobilizing churches to pray 24/7 for unity and revival in Austin, Texas! Today about 100 churches pray 24/7 for Austin to be transformed. You can read about this story in *City of Prayer: Transform Your Community through Praying Churches*, which Trey co-wrote with Dr. Kie Bowman. Trey also wrote *Revival Cry: Contending for Transformation in This Generation*.

## Mary Anne Kent

As a little girl, Mary Anne believed she would one day become a pastor's wife and missionary. When she fell in love with a tennis playing theology student in college, the fulfillment of her childhood dream began. Trey and Mary Anne married in 1985 soon after her college graduation and began a life of ministry and adventure. This adventure took them to Austin, Texas in 1993 where they planted and continue to serve at Northwest Fellowship. Mary Anne enjoyed teaching school for many years until she decided to take her love of encouraging, equipping and motivating to the church where she joyfully serves in women's ministry. She also enjoys the opportunity to minister on worship and prayer teams, encourage pastors' wives, motivate women's groups, and share Jesus in any way, any place and with anyone God allows. Prayer is the heartbeat and foundation of her life and she loves to motivate others to talk to Jesus. She is blessed to have been married to her hero, sweetheart and best friend, Trey, for 35 years and is amazed and grateful to be the mother to two beautiful adult daughters, Lindsay and Christina, the proud mother-in-law to Christina's husband, Nick and the "over-the-moon-in-love" grandmother to Samuel David and Levi John.

# Imagine if Hundreds of Intercessors Would Pray for Your City!

Why not put copies of *Praying God's Word Over Your City* in the hands of your friends and congregation? God might use you to raise up an army to pray for your community.

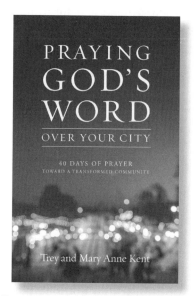

Multiple Copy Discounts Available at **prayershop.org**

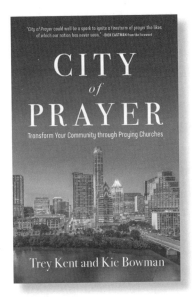

# *Prayer*CONNECT

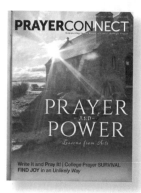  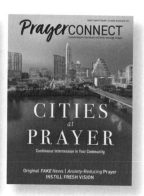

## A QUARTERLY MAGAZINE DESIGNED TO:

**Mobilize believers** to pray God's purposes for
their church, city and nation.

**Connect intercessors** with the growing worldwide prayer movement.

**Equip prayer leaders and pastors** with tools
to disciple their congregations.

**Each issue of *Prayer Connect* includes:**
- Practical articles to equip and inspire your
  prayer life.
- Helpful prayer tips and proven ideas.
- News of prayer movements around the world.
- Theme articles exploring important prayer topics.
- Connections to prayer resources available online.

**Print subscription: $24.99**
(includes digital version)

**Digital subscription: $19.99**

**Church Prayer Leaders Network
membership: $35.99** (includes print,
digital, and CPLN membership benefits)

## SUBSCRIBE NOW.
www.prayerleader.com/membership or call 800-217-5200